DARLING MUTTI

A Jacana Book

DARLING MUTTI

edited & compiled by Joan Marshall

Related titles by Jacana:

The Dreamcloth
African Soul Talk
Boerejood
A Life of One's Own

First published in 2005 by
Jacana Media (Pty) Ltd.
10 Orange Street
Sunnyside 2092
Johannesburg
South Africa

ISBN 1-77009-166-1

Photographs by the author
Author's photograph by Harold Marshall
Cover design: Michiel Botha
Set in: Ehrhardt 12/15
Printed and bound by CTP Printers, Cape Town

See a complete list of Jacana titles at www.jacana.co.za

CONTENTS

THANKS

TO THE EDITORIAL STAFF at Jacana Media and especially to Maggie Davey who made the decision to publish the book and to the editor and Serusha Govender for all their help. To Marion Scher and Susan Sandler for the introduction. To my friend, Brenda Finkelstein, who was the first to read and edit my manuscript many years ago. To Ann Lundt who had the difficult task of translating my mother's stained and often illegible tiny German diaries. But most of all, to my beloved husband, Harold, without whose encouragement over the years the stories of Gerda, Kurt and Edith would never have seen the light of day.

DEDICATION

THIS BOOK IS DEDICATED to the memory of my beloved parents, Fritz and Gerda Herrmann, who gave Ronny, Fay and me a wonderfully happy childhood.

FOREWORD

MY MOTHER KNEW she was going to die. On Friday, 9 October 1987, we went for a short walk before dinner. She had not been feeling too well for a couple of weeks and was due to see a heart specialist the following week for a check-up.

While we were strolling along she told me that she had ordered hand-made crocodile skin handbags for my sister and my birthdays and needed to tell me about them in case she was no longer alive when they arrived as I would have to pay for them from her estate. Fay's was a belated gift as my mother had gone on what she called a 'farewell' trip to all her family in America, Israel and England in July/August and had not been here to celebrate with Fay on her birthday. Besides these two ominous facts, she had also already warned me that after her death I was to go through all the pockets of her clothes and her handbags to check that there was no money there before disposing of her things. I was also instructed on the future of her cat. When she died we would have to very carefully catch the cat, put her in a cage and take her to the vet to be euthanised as the cat was so spoilt that nobody else would be able to live with it. She loved that animal who was, indeed, the most vicious and spoilt cat on earth!

My mother was a hoarder but only after her death did I actually learn the full extent of this!

She never, ever, threw away a plastic bag! There were hundreds and hundreds of carrier bags in a cupboard in her kitchen as well as transparent plastic bags that had been used, washed and saved for another day.

She also never threw away any mail. I spent hours sitting on her bed going through mounds of already opened post which had been carefully put back into the envelopes and kept after she had read them. Most of these envelopes contained pamphlets, notices, and special offers for old expired events.

And then, I found the letter addressed to my brother, sister and me. Usually cool, calm and collected, I went to pieces after reading this letter. My husband, Harold, had to leave his office, drive to my mother's apartment and sit with me until I was once again in control of myself. I have included this letter in the book so that you can try to imagine yourself in my place, unexpectedly getting a letter like this from your beloved mother three weeks after her death.

Two days later I found four little journals my mother had started writing more than four years after she first arrived in South Africa from Germany, and had them translated. They contained letters to her mother, my grandmother, who was still in Germany trying in vain to obtain a visa to come to South Africa. Harold so enjoyed reading my mother's letters to her mother that he nagged and nagged until I sat down and wrote my mother's story. This is what you hold now. I have also included the stories of Kurt Herrmann, my father's first cousin, and Edith Twelkemeier Forrester, his niece, whose lives were also indelibly affected by the events in Germany in the period leading up to, and during, World War II.

It has taken 18 years for this book to become a reality.

INTRODUCTION

WHEN JOAN MARSHALL uncovered her mother's journals she began to unravel a moving story of a family deeply affected by the Holocaust. Told in part by the recollections of three cousins, their stories span generations and reveal the heartbreaking truths of the suffering and isolation experienced by those German Jews who survived the Holocaust but were separated from their loved ones.

Their tale begins with Gerda Herrmann, Joan's mother, who manages to flee Nazi Germany and emigrates to South Africa. While slowly adapting to her new life in Cape Town she patiently awaits the arrival of her beloved parents from Germany. Because she is unable to contact them she writes to them in her journals, hoping that some day she will be able to share her experiences with them.

Meanwhile, as the Nazis tear apart the Jewish community, seven-year-old Edith Twelkemeier Forrester is evacuated to Scotland from Germany on one of the many Kindertransports, a desperate step many Jewish people took in order to send their children to safety, hoping to be reunited with them later. Adopted by a generous Scottish couple she grows up separated from the family she loved and at the age of fourteen discovers the truth about her parents' fate.

And drawing the strands of their family history together is the story of Kurt Herrmann. After enduring much terror and hardship to escape capture by the Gestapo he was able to emigrate to the United States and served in the intelligence corps during World War II. His story tells of his family's experiences in the period leading up to the War, and his search for his beloved parents thereafter. His revelations bring together their trials and heartaches and paints a rare, insightful picture of the repercussions of Nazi Germany that few are aware of.

LIST OF PHOTOGRAPHS

1. Joan Marshall (3 months old). February 1941
2. Hannie and Jackie Mailich with Gerda and baby Joan
3. Heinie and Jackie Mailich with Gerda and baby Joan
4. Herrmann family. December 1953
5. Herrmann family. Port Elizabeth, December 1948
6. Joan, Ronnie and Fay Herrmann. December 1948
7. Gerda in Berlin. Circa 1936
8. Gerda and Joan at Joan's wedding. 6 February 1965
9. Joan's grandmother. December 1936
10. Solomon and Bertha Mailich (Gerda's parents). Berlin, 1935
11. Full-size extract from Gerda's diary
12. Gerda in Berlin. Circa 1935
13. Gerda, Fritz (right) and friends on the 'SS Duilio' coming to South Africa, 1936
14. Gerda, Fritz and friend on the 'SS Duilio' coming to South Africa, 1936
15. Gerda on honeymoon. July 1938
16. Gerda and Fritz with baby Joan. January 1941

17. Gerda with Joan, Ronnie and Fay. October 1948
18. Fritz with Joan. January 1943
19. Fritz, Gerda and Joan. November 1942
20. Gerda entertaining guests at her silver wedding anniversary with Joan in the background. July 1963
21. Gerda and Fritz. August 1970
22. Gerda, the last picture taken before her death. August 1987
23. Extract from Gerda's diary.
24. Herrmann family. September 1961
25. Joan Marshall. December 2004
26. Letter from the South African Red Cross Society
27. Edith Twelkemeier in Scotland. Undated
28. Edith as a young woman. Undated
29. Edith as a young woman. Undated
30. Edith with Kurt and Ursula Herrmann in Los Angeles.
31. Unknown newspaper clipping showing Edith disembarking from the Kindertransport with other children.
32. Young Edith with her parents and grandmother
33. Edith while visiting South Africa. Undated
34. Kurt Herrmann, 1945
35. Kurt at age 87 Los Angeles. Spring 2005
36. Kurt and Joan in Los Angeles. Spring 2005

GERDA'S STORY

Introduction

MY MOTHER, GERDA HERRMANN, could have been featured in the *Readers Digest* series 'My Most Unforgettable Character'! She had a lust for life and a capacity for overcoming every difficulty and obstacle which was, truly, quite remarkable. She was full of life, full of fun and full of love, which she shared so generously with her family and friends. She was quick-tempered and volatile but returned to her normal good humour as fast as she lost it. Life with my mother was never dull or boring.

My father, Fritz Herrmann, was the complete opposite. A gentleman to his fingertips, slow to anger, courteous to a fault and so very proud of his wife and children. A small-town boy, one sometimes had the feeling that he couldn't quite believe that he was actually married to this exotic butterfly but was enjoying the experience!

This unlikely couple was happily married for over 34 years and had three children. I am the oldest and then four years later my brother, Ronnie, was born, followed two years after that by our sister, Fay.

My parents were both born in the part of Germany which was later to become East Germany. My mother was born and bred in 1912 in decadent Berlin, while my father, born in 1902, came from a small town called Nordhausen. Both came from close-knit families with similar backgrounds and were observant rather than religious Orthodox Jews.

My dad had a brother, Walter, who emigrated to America in 1936 and a sister, Erna, who died in Auschwitz. My grandfather passed away in 1917 and my paternal grandmother died of cancer in 1937. My mom was from a smaller family and had one brother, Heinz, or Heini as he was affectionately known.

My mother's emigration from Germany, although traumatic for her family, was relatively simple. She had completed her apprenticeship and was newly qualified as a dressmaker. It was becoming extremely dangerous for Jews in Germany and most people applied for visas to emigrate to safe countries, such as Britain, America, Israel and South Africa. In April 1936, with the owner of Foschini's dress shop in South Africa guaranteeing her a job as an alteration hand, passage to Cape Town was booked and paid for, clothes packed and with the equivalent of ten pounds in her purse, accompanied by her beloved parents, she took the train to Hamburg where they would see their beloved daughter safely on board the ship to her new life at the furthest point on the Dark Continent of Africa where she would attempt to get sponsors for her family so they could join her in South Africa.

In contrast, my father's emigration was fraught with danger. He was an engineer employed in a highly sensitive position by a large company which was engaged in designing and manufacturing ammunition, amongst other things. He lived and worked in the town of Zuhl and had gone home to Nordhausen in March 1936, on his annual leave. He told us that, as a Jewish person he had to report in to a police station once a week and after seven days leave he went to the one nearest his mother's house. The policeman on duty happened to be a school friend of his brother's and he warned my father not to go back to work when his leave was up as he would be sent to a concentration camp due the knowledge he possessed of highly confidential armaments.

One can only imagine what went on in the life of this family over the next two weeks. No place to go, no guarantee of a job to get him into a friendly country and, worst of all, no passport! Drastic steps had to be taken, an application for a passport was made and passage booked on the first ship to leave Germany for a friendly country after the estimated arrival of this passport. There was no time to apply to any country for a visa and he discovered that the 'SS Duilio' was leaving for South Africa and decided that this was where he was going. He hoped that something would happen to make him an acceptable immigrant.

The passport arrived the morning he was due to leave for Hamburg to board his ship to South Africa and he said goodbye to his brother and sister and beloved niece, Edith. He set off with his mother to spend his last night in Germany. The only member of his family he ever saw again was Edith, who traced him in 1961. She was sent out of Germany to Britain by the Red Cross on a Kindertransport at the age of seven and was fostered, and later adopted, by a wonderful Scottish couple, the Forresters. Twenty-four years later Edith was able to share her terrifying and horrifying stories with her long-lost uncle.

The night before the 'Duilio' was due to set sail, both families went to the theatre. During the interval Fritz spotted Gerda sitting with her parents and he turned to his mother and said, 'You see that girl over there? Now that is the kind of girl I would like to marry!' My grand-mother was horrified and exclaimed, 'But she is wearing make-up!'

The next day, after all the goodbyes had been said and the ship had left Germany, Fritz suddenly caught a glimpse of the very girl he had seen at the theatre the night before. He introduced himself and a romance was born.

He still did not have a job waiting for him in South Africa and deporta-tion back to Germany was sure to follow when he arrived in Cape Town without any papers, but he was young and full of hope for the future.

One night, while sitting with a group of shipmates, he met an American who was sailing to Port Elizabeth to open a tyre factory. When this man heard that my father was an engineer he immediately offered him a job with his company, Firestone, and gave him sponsorship papers to work in South Africa while still on the ship. This job was to last a lifetime.

The path of true love never runs smoothly. My mother disembarked in Cape Town where her new life was to begin, while my father had to carry on to Port Elizabeth a distance of some 1075 kilometres.

My mother enjoyed her life in Cape Town, had a very active social life, was extremely popular and had quite a few marriage proposals, which she turned down, as she was in love with my father. My father worked very hard at Firestone, first helping with the building of the factory and offices and then becoming the maintenance foreman of the factory. He was earning a good salary and managed to buy himself a car and was able to drive down to Cape Town to visit my mother every few months.

Two years after arriving in South Africa, on 3 July 1938, my parents were married and settled down in a new home in Port Elizabeth.

During this time my mother had not been idle. She had managed to get a guarantee for her parents to come and live in South Africa from the owner of a bicycle store in Loeb Street, Cape Town. My grandfather and uncle were both specialists in the repair and maintenance of bicycles and motorbikes so this was the ideal position for them.

However, my grandparents felt they would rather have their young son, Heinz, and his wife safely out of Germany. They had applied for entry into the United States but this had not yet been successful and by now it was extremely dangerous for Jews to remain in Germany. Once my uncle and aunt arrived in South Africa, my mother and her brother started trying to find ways and means of getting another guarantee to get their parents into South Africa before time ran out and the country's quota for Jewish immigrants was filled.

South Africa closed its doors to Jewish immigrants in 1938 but my mother never gave up trying to get the papers that would save her parents' lives. In 1942 she was somehow informed that her parents were coming to South Africa.

I was too young to understand or remember any of these events but during my early years some pieces of my grandparents' luggage – a grandfather clock and a wooden box with some linen, cutlery and crockery arrived.

And Gerda waited and waited and waited not knowing that her beloved parents, Solomon and Bertha Mailich, had already been painfully and cruelly executed by the Nazis in Auschwitz.

After my mother's death in 1987 I found four little diaries which were translated for me by my friend and neighbour, Ann Lund.

To me this account of my life, before my birth and for a few months after, is a treasure made even more precious by the knowledge that my grandmother never did get to read these loving letters so carefully preserved for 47 years.

Gerda's diaries
Book I

Port Elizabeth, South Africa
4th August, 1940

My beloved Mutti,
I bought this little book specially to be able to talk to you and to give you to read so that you may know that you are, and were, always with me in my thoughts.

I am now at the beginning of my seventh month and we are hoping the baby will come in October. I wonder whether you know this yet and if my letters are reaching you!

Müttischen, we have really tried everything to get you both to South Africa but always encounter new obstacles. We could possibly get you to China but now I cannot get any money out of South Africa and even in China things don't look too good for the Jews. Our hands are really tied! And how much I need you.

Fritz is wonderful, Mutti, and I love him very, very much. He looks after me and does not want me to go on working. I should like to stop soon. I get tired sitting at the sewing machine and should like to stay well.

Do you know, Mutti, that I always talk to you in my mind – oh Olle – if only you were here!

Up to now I am still very slender, so much sits 'behind', I have not grown broader and my face is unchanged. Most people say I have grown prettier and will have a son; I don't mind – a girl will be just as welcome!

I just hope that if it is a boy he will look like Fritz as he is really handsome. Fritz just laughs! Or it will be red-haired, as Papa has red hair, and I have always wanted a red-haired child! Enough for today, shall write again soon.

Lovingly,
Your Gerda

8th August, 1940

Dearest Mutti,
Yesterday I received such pretty presents! Three pastel baby jackets, really fabulous, first-rate articles of the very best wool – so sweet! I also got two pairs of knitted pants and half a dozen booties. One of my customers, Mrs Bertwhistle, made them. I am not superstitious and do not think one should not starting preparing a trousseau in advance. Are you superstitious?

Yesterday I bought material for napkins and nighties but it was very expensive. So – no more! By the way, I shall be going to the doctor again on Monday – I go every month – and I hope my heart will be better. I think we drink our coffee too strong! I drank <u>100</u> cups in 14 days!

Loving kisses,
Gerda

9th August, 1940

Good morning, Mutti!

I hope you are feeling well and not worrying about us. According to the latest newspaper reports, Herr Hitler is talking as though the war was already won! I hope you will not worry! We very firmly believe that England will win otherwise there is no justice and nor is there your *Liebe G'tt*!

I am sorry that we don't live in the same town as my brother and his family but it cannot be altered. I sent Heini's little boy, Jackie, a charming blue suit and Hanni a dress.

14th August, 1940

Darling Mutti,
Yesterday I went to the doctor. I had to go every four weeks and from now on I have to go every fourteen days. He was very satisfied with me. My heart is in order again and my lungs completely healthy. The baby's position is normal and he says its heart is exceptionally strong. I am really glad. I am just a little nervous and on top of this I can never ask you anything! The doctor says my nipples are not good – too small. I am watching this and doing everything to enlarge them.

Today I am going to my lady doctor. I like going to her, I can talk to her just as I would to you and ask all the silly questions I want to. I did not have any internal examinations after the first time which was to establish whether I was pregnant. So, Mutti, till later, by the way, the doctor says the baby can come any time up to the 19th November. He says with a first child one can never be sure!

As I mentioned, yesterday I went to the lady doctor. There was nothing special. We just chatted. I want to do a course in baby care.

Unfortunately, there is an infection in the baby clinic at the moment so I shall have to wait and see what happens.

Today, or rather even yesterday, I did not feel well at all. I had indigestion and, above all, today I was terribly giddy. I am better again!

But I was so amused about Fritz! Just as I got back from the doctor and told him the baby is so well positioned and its heart beating so strongly, a visitor arrived and I went out quickly to make coffee. Through the door I could follow the conversation between Fritz and Mr Findling and I heard how proudly Fritz told him about the baby and how well it is lying, etc. I wished I could've kissed him there and then! I found it so sweet – you too?

31st August, 1940

My dearest Müttischen, I have not written for a long time as there was nothing new.

There isn't anything new today but, Mutti, I have a terrible longing for you!

I have been back to the doctor. I am still going fortnightly. He is satisfied with me; everything is in good order. Well, another one and a half to two months and then everything will be over. I received some booties from a friend, really beautifully made! I am often tired now, especially in the afternoons and I am changing too – such glassy eyes and a red face – isn't it strange?

Mutti, it is possible that we shall be moving. The landlord is not prepared to reduce the rent and I thought well, either, or, and so far he says he will accept our notice. I am not very enthusiastic and am curious to know what Fritz will say when he gets home.

It was Fritz's birthday on Thursday, 38 years old! We heard that Heini will have to go to army camp in the next few days. My poor brother! We know Berlin was bombed during the last few days. I hope you have not had to suffer because of this and that you are alright. I am glad you all know how Goebbels lies!

Kisses and greetings,
Gerda

Meine Kleine,

Today I am rather worried because we went out on Saturday night and I slipped and have very strong pains in my body. Above all I worry because the baby moved so exceptionally strongly on Sunday. On Sunday I felt quite well – but the night from Sunday to Monday was awful, I could not sleep. I am going to the doctor early. I hope everything is all right.

I meant to tell you before, Fritz has spoken calmly to our landlord and we are now staying on in this flat. I am quite glad!

Today I packed my little case with my things and the things for the baby. I have rinsed out everything and I am now sewing some nighties.

Heini is already in camp. Hanni would like to move here from Cape Town, if it is possible.

Well, Olle, I'll tell you what the doctor said later.

10th September, 1940

Dear Müttischen,

You need not be uneasy. I went to the doctor and he examined me thoroughly and, thank goodness, everything is fine. He thinks I may have pulled a muscle but did not harm the baby. Isn't that good? He says my heart is fine, so is the baby's and that it moves so much is understandable. It needs practice as it is older now.

When I got back Fritz was home from work and waiting on the balcony. He came down quickly to hear whether all was well.

Yesterday I visited my friend Lotte in the hospital. She had a baby boy eight days ago. I looked at all the babies and to me they all looked the same – small, red, wrinkled – but sweet! Lotte naturally asserted that her baby was the best behaved and prettiest of all the babies but I think all mothers think that! I am feeling fine, only my hands get pins and needles. I have had to take off all my rings, even the wedding ring, as my fingers have become so swollen. When I get up in the morning I think every finger is as fat as a sausage.

Yesterday we received the second letter from Heini. I shall write to him twice every week.

So kleine Mutz – I must get dressed. It is eight o'clock in the morning. In my mind I give you a big kiss!

Mutti, I weighed myself at the butcher as a joke! The scale showed 135 lb! Before I was pregnant I was 108 lb. Quite something, isn't it?

Yesterday I went to the doctor again. Everything is fine although I have really not felt very well this week and have had cramp round the eyes and mouth. I am even heavier and feel very clumsy, particularly in bed. By the way, I am wearing the nighties you gave me, Mutti!

I baked a mocha cake for Heini. It was a lot of work and I was exhausted afterwards.

Hanni is coming to visit but we don't know exactly when. She is coming at rather an awkward time for me. I am always rather tired and so I am a little afraid of Jackie although he seems to be a sweet little boy, judging by the pictures and Heini's songs of praise!

By the way, Mutti, I shall probably have a nurse for eight to ten days after coming out of hospital. Fritz feels this will be right. He says he will have more peace of mind if he knows that I will have some rest. We asked Hanni to help but she says she has to take care of Jackie because 'the little one needs all her attention'. Oh, Müttischen mein, if only you were here! Now there are only four to six weeks to wait until the baby comes! We will send a telegram via America. I hope you will receive it!

Loving greetings,
Your Gerda

By the way, I received two beautiful bibs from Mrs Salinger. She crocheted them herself. Yesterday Mrs Kahan brought me one and a half pounds of homemade chocolates. Decent of them wasn't it?

Meine Süsse, today is the second day of Rosh Hashanah and I am thinking of you both constantly and know that your thoughts are with us. I did not go to the Temple as Fritz had to work and it was too taxing for me to go alone.

I have recently become pretty sturdy, my legs, particularly, are swelling up badly. I hope this will improve afterwards. Hanni will be coming in the next fortnight. I am glad that you do not know that Heini is a sol- dier – you would only worry! The baby pushes against me a lot. I have to sit up very straight.

So, Müttischen, I wish you a healthy New Year and that we may soon be together again!

On Tuesday I shall be going to the doctor again.

Gerda

Today is Monday, October 7th and here in South Africa it is a holiday! Why, I do not know! Fritz has to work, unfortunately. Next week I am expecting Hanni to arrive. Yesterday we had stuffed Milz for dinner – outstanding! But the work!

On Saturday it will be Yom Kippur. I hope Fritz will not have to work but because of the war he may have to.

The baby is growing nicely. I am very, very well except for the swollen legs. I am happy and feel well. Fritz says no-one notices anything from the back, but I think my figure looks like a blown-up balloon! So, Müttischen, Book I has come to an end and I shall start another one. In the next diary there will certainly be something about the baby for, from now on, I only have three to four weeks left.

Book II

Meine Süsse Mutz, I am now starting the second book to you. Today is Erev Yom Kippur and earlier I had a great deal to do with all the cooking, etc. Fritz will be staying at home tomorrow and I am so happy. We shall not be going to shul as we cannot afford the seats and in the very orthodox community we do not understand one word.

Besides, I cannot stand the stuffy, bad air in there.

On Wednesday I was at the doctor's. Everything is fine. Before he examined me he said he did not think that I would have the baby before the 12th or 15th of November. After he examined me he said that possibly it would be earlier in the month as the baby is very active and everything seems to indicate that I will soon be ready. I am very glad, for now that it is so hot it is not pleasant with my fat tummy!

Today I washed curtains. The sun burns everything. Oh, Mutti, they ripped to shreds!

So, my darling, I should like to wish you and Papa only the best for Yom Kippur and I think of everything good for you both. We think of you a great deal. Well, that you can imagine.

Once again, everything, everything good!
Your Gerda

Today I am sitting up in bed in hospital and am writing you. I have been here since twelve o'clock last night and am waiting eagerly to see whether 'it' is really going to arrive or whether it is a false alarm.

I had bad pains, which stopped the moment I got to the hospital! Now I have pains again but I have no idea whether these are birth pangs; I doubt it! Fritz has been here already. He is so sweet.

I have just eaten breakfast and vomited up everything immediately.

It is nine o'clock. I do not feel well but they do not think it is time yet.

Fritz has just been here again. It is almost one o'clock. The poor man is looking very bad. Just imagine Mutti, the doctor was here while I was asleep and he didn't wake me. It is very boring here in the hospital and I think I shall be able to go home later.

It is two o'clock now. Next door someone is having a baby. It is dreadful to listen to and makes me quite weak. I would really like to block my ears. I still have bad pains but, unfortunately, not the right ones. I wanted to do my hair so that I would look better but the moaning is making me weak and nervous.

Half past two. The woman has had her baby, her fifth child! The baby arrived in barely five minutes but before it was born I thought the woman was being tortured! I think it is not a pleasure to have a baby! I have one wish – that I shall not scream!

Five o'clock. I am still in hospital. They want me to wait until Fritz comes before getting dressed. I can't lie still any more!

24th October, 1940

That was a false alarm and I am still waiting. I am lying in bed at home, I have the feeling that the baby might be early, that would be nice, exactly on your wedding anniversary. I hope for that so much. I have been poorly for almost ten days, I can't walk.

So loving kisses, I am lying very uncomfortably,
Your Gerda

6th November, 1940

Meine Süsse, the baby is still not here! We're already quite nervous. For three weeks I was really not well but for the past two days I have been feeling better.
Hanni and Jackie have been here with us for the past three weeks. Jackie is the exact image of Heini, a charming, pretty boy, you would be very proud! They have been staying in a furnished house for three days as it became too much for me.
I am nervous and Hanni even more so – and then there was little Jackie! It wasn't nice and the work was too much for the maid so she stopped coming. Luckily Hanni and I understand each other very well. I hope it stays that way.

Mutti, I have a baby's wicker crib all ready. Everything goes well and the baby is healthy. So, Mutz, enough chatter!

Your daughter, who thinks of you constantly, kisses you lovingly,
Gerda

7th November, 1940

Oh Mutti, I am so unhappy! I had pains the whole night, real birth pains which came every hour. I didn't sleep and then early this morning, at half past six, they stopped and then I had a note from the maid to say that she cannot come, she is sick. Now I have to get up and wash the dishes and make the beds and I do feel so awful I could cry!

9th November, 1940

Still without a baby and a maid – both enough to make one despair. My health is much better again and I can walk once more. Müttischen, just now a maid was here looking for a job. She seems very nice and will start tomorrow, Sunday. I am very glad for I was worried about what would become of my home while I was in hospital. If only the baby would come! I am sure it is going to be a boy as I carry everything in my tummy right at the front.

Loving kisses,
Your Gerda

Muttili, the maid is already working and seems to be nice. She works slowly but everything is sparkling. Fritz has a great deal of work. He works from six-thirty in the morning until eight at night almost daily, even on Sundays. I am not very enthusiastic about it. He earns well at the expense of his health. I am very well but alas, no sign of the baby. I have to sleep sitting up at night because my tummy presses down so hard but I sleep well although I wake up fairly often.

Kissing you,
Gerda

18th November, 1940

Beloved, precious Mutti, Baby is here at last! And you have a grand-daughter! We are blissfully happy. On Saturday, the sixteenth of November at one-thirty in the afternoon, the little rascal arrived!
On Saturday morning at six-thirty, Fritz took me to the hospital. I had strong contractions and at ten o'clock things really started.
At the end I was given chloroform and regained consciousness fully at about two-thirty because Fritz appeared then. Before that I couldn't come around properly but the sight of my dearest husband was the best medicine. At four o'clock they brought us the baby. Mutti – too sweet, with quite long black hair – almost an Eton crop – with a cocks-comb in the middle and blue eyes. And my chin, just as pointed. And Mutti, my fingers. The hands, I mean the shapes of the nails, are exactly like yours. Oh how you would love the baby and so would Papa! I have not dared to kiss her yet. I have just put my face against hers for she is so delicate. Lotte was the first visitor and wanted to see the child and asked the nurse which one was Baby Herrmann. The nurse said: 'The prettiest

baby here' and Lotte has given me her word that that is so! Hanni is also totally enthusiastic! Better not ask what Fritz and I think!

Enough – here comes Baby so END.

Most lovingly, your happy,
Gerda

22nd November, 1940

Today little Joan is six days old but she still does not understand how to take the breast. It is a battle every time. Mutti, I have so much milk that it is unbelievable. I could feed three children with ease. They draw off approximately 5 ounces every time as Baby gets enough from one side. She is sweet. Resemblance is still difficult to determine, only your nails exactly, my fingers and chin.

We are both **so** happy we are bursting with joy!

14th December, 1940

I have been home for fourteen days and today our little Joan Ellen is four weeks old. I am still a little weak on my feet.

20th January, 1941

Couldn't write more last time. Muttili, the little one is sweet. You would be ecstatic. We are also so proud. She weighs 10 pounds at two months and has grown into a real little girl. I shall write more in my next letter.

Loving kisses
Your Gerda

Book III

Mutti, your little grandchild is sleeping peacefully on the balcony. She looks so enchanting that I have to keep going to look in on her! At the moment we have a visitor who would make you happy – your friend, Martha Roth, with her grandson. Tante Martha will also write in here. I am looking forward to the time when you will read it all!

Kisses,
Gerda

Now just look at this! I am with your beloved Gerda and Fritz! Both invited me so warmly and I am enjoying the happiness of the young Mother and Father. Both are very proud of the baby, and rightly so, it is as pretty as a picture, healthy and delightful. Every day brings something new and I have just one wish – that it may be granted to you to see all the children together soon.

In love and friendship,
Your Martha

15th March, 1941

Mutti,
On the 1st of March I had a letter from Ruth Abrahams in America. She writes that she sent you a telegram. I wrote to you and sent a picture of us and one of the baby. I hope you will receive it.

Mummy our Joanie is the sweetest baby you can imagine, pretty as a picture (and that's no exaggeration), and always laughing. Oh, how much I wish I could introduce you to your little grandchild soon. She is four months old now and weighs 13 pounds.

9th May, 1941

Today I want to write a few words again. Joan will be six months next week and is sweet! She is already having trouble teething and does not want to eat. I am still breastfeeding her – isn't that excellent?

I hope you will receive the picture I sent via Ruth. I also want to send one picture via China. Our treasure can almost sit up. She would dearly love to stand! At the moment she is lying next to me and is telling herself long stories – quite enchanting! Fritz and I are wonderfully happy with her and only you are missing!

3rd July, 1941

Today I have been married for three years and that's why my ears are ringing! You will certainly be thinking of us! You know, Mutti, when you are among strangers no-one remembers that it is your anniversary but what wouldn't <u>you</u> have done for us at home! Well, I suppose it isn't too bad after all; I am just so fond of celebrating!

Mutti, our little *Putzelschen* can say 'Mama' already – she just babbles it to herself and I could hug her! She is crawling on the ground now and looks too sweet. She wears long pull-on pants like a sturdy little boy. She has an incredible temperament and always makes me think of myself for she shouts for joy – just as I used to do. She looks exactly like me, has the same eyes, only they are blue and, if possible, more sparkling than mine. She loves eating oranges, although she pulls terrible faces as they are probably a little sour, but she gets quite excited when she sees a slice of orange. She gets a piece of bread at midday which she eats with enormous enjoyment and it is lovely to see how she concentrates when she pushes it into her mouth and chews on it. If it falls out of her hand she looks for it and often puts her hand on top of it by mistake and then she can't see it – then Mommy has to come quickly and help her to look for it! She's so good and sweet!

I am sitting at the table eating my lunch, reading and writing to you. Joanie is playing on the floor with empty boxes, etc. We go to the park every afternoon and I have to keep watching her as she loves to crawl to the flower beds and put sand in her mouth. She is always cheerful, but does not like getting dressed to go home in the afternoon. I generally take my time dressing her but it gets cold by five o'clock and I want to get home in good time so I do not laugh and play as much with her and this does not suit her at all.

She sleeps wonderfully well; by seven o'clock at night I switch off the light and don't hear another sound from her. At the moment I am still waking her up between ten and eleven at night to feed her and so that she can play with her Daddy (who is *meshugga* about her.) She 'crows' for a little while, I switch off the light, go to bed and our daughter sleeps until Fritz's alarm goes off the next morning. I change her and feed her again and she goes back to sleep until about nine o'clock. At ten o'clock she eats then she sleeps from eleven to twelve-thirty. Isn't that prima? After that we go out if the weather is fine and then madame sleeps for another half hour during her stroll in the pram. So, Olle, no more today.

Loving kisses,
Gerda

7th July, 1941

Beloved Olle, my wedding anniversary is now four days behind me. Heini and Hanni forgot about it! In the afternoon I went to the confectioners for tea with my daughter, who slept in her pram the whole time we were there. Fritz gave me really beautiful gladioli. Yes and that was my third wedding anniversary. Our *Putzelchen* is sweet. When she is lying in bed she always pulls her blanket over her face and then when I say, 'Where is my baby?' she quickly pulls it away from her face. She sometimes does that ten times or more!

Kisses for you Mutti, from 'Mama'

10th July, 1941

Müttischen, Joan has her first tooth! I discovered it today – that is, just now. A lovely moment! I rushed out quickly to tell my maid. At home I would have phoned you but here I must do it this way! (I mean writing to you instead of phoning.)

Lovingly
Me

Since I last wrote to you Joan has two little teeth, can sit alone and is altogether 'big' already. She holds on to the railing of her cot and stands quite steadily. Yesterday I went to the cafe to have tea and Joanie sat on the chair next to me and I was so proud. It's quite something for an eight-month-old baby! For the past two days she has had vegetables for lunch although I still breastfeed her fully. I want her to get used to food gradually before I wean her completely.

She bites me now!

So, Mutti, I hope that you can feel that we think of you constantly and speak about you. I have such a terrible longing for you and in thought I ask your advice about everything!

Kisses,
Gerda

30th July, 1941

Good Morning Mami! Hearty congratulations on your birthday! I have just one wish and that is that you and Papa are well and that you will have many years to enjoy your children and grandchildren! Joan is sitting on my lap, hence the scrawl.

I dreamt about you last night! Isn't that fine? More later.

Loving kisses,
Your Gerda

21st September, 1941

Today is Erev Rosh Hashanah and I want to wish you both, all the best. Müttischen, I hope this year will bring us together.

Joan is sweet, now ten months and has eight teeth. I am very tired, had guests, it is twelve o'clock at night. I shall write more later.

Loving kisses from your Fritz, Gerda, and Joan

23rd September, 1941

My most dearly beloved ones, today is the second day of Rosh Hashanah. Fritz has to work but he was off yesterday. Baby is fabulous. At less than nine months she already managed to pull herself up to stand. Now she stands and falls everywhere and can pull herself around in her playpen. She has eight teeth, which are already very big, says 'Papa' and 'Mama', claps her hands, waves when one says 'Ta-ta', is very friendly and is always laughing and goes to anyone. She babbles all day in her own baby language and if she likes something she clicks her tongue, it sounds too sweet. I always regret it so much that you do not know this sweet child. She would make you very happy.

So, my two loved ones, once again I shall end this. By the way, Mutti, I celebrated your birthday. I invited a friend and her two children to go to the confectioners with me. Oh, if only you could come here soon. It would be too lovely.

So now to close,
Loving kisses, your Gerda

I have not written to you for a long time but I have thought of you all the time, Mutti, and I dream of both of you constantly.

Joan is now almost one year and two months and is so sweet! We had a great celebration for her first birthday. The guests started arriving at ten o'clock in the morning. In the afternoon there were 25 people here for coffee. She has been walking for a long time now.

4th May, 1942

Again my letter has lain unwritten for a while and now I want to tell you how sweet Joanie is. We have specially had some pictures taken of her and have made a film so that you will be able to see her properly later. When she sees your pictures she says 'Omi' and 'Opi' and copies every-thing we say. We have to speak English so that she doesn't copy all the German. She is a very pretty child (that's what Fritz and I think) but actually everyone says 'like a doll'. At one and a half years Joan has 16 teeth. That's good, isn't it? She has never been sick, thank goodness but has diarrhoea at the moment and is very pale. You should see how loving the little scamp is. She cuddles up to us or with us when she really means it and says, 'Oh G'd, Oh G'd, Oh G'd'! When we tickle her she says, 'killa killa killi killi killi'. You could eat her up, it sounds so sweet.

But if she sees that I am cross she strokes my face, turns her little face to one side and says, 'ooh'.

Muttilein, today is your 60th birthday and we are thinking of you very intensely. Actually I had meant to have a big celebration but I have a very bad cold and guests would be too exhausting. So we are going to the cinema.

Oh Mutti, I dream of you constantly. If only you were here already.

Joan is sweet. She says 'Oma' and 'Opa' to your pictures. She is 20 months old and speaks like a child of at least two and a half – quite enchanting. When she wants something she says 'Give it to Joanie' or 'Joanie wants' and always says 'thank you'. If she is sorry about something she says 'oh shame' or 'sorry'. She has a doll's pram and loves her 'baba' very much. Then she stands and rocks her doll to and fro. I could eat her up! So, Mamilein, I hope that you are well, that is my constant prayer and it is the wish of all of us that we have you here with us soon.

So, my beloved, I want to bake a cake for you. Fritz will be home by four o'clock and then we will have birthday cake.

Loving kisses,
Your Gerda

I actually hear you speak.

11th September, 1942
Rosh Hashanah

Dearly beloved parents – sadly another festival without you. I could cry all the time. If only the war were over and we had you here! I expect your longing is just as great. We speak about you constantly. Tonight is Erev Rosh Hashanah and the Salingers are coming to dinner. Fritz will not be working tomorrow.

Joanie is so sweet and gives us so much joy, she speaks too adorably.

Next month I am going to Heini and Hanni in Johannesburg for fourteen days. I am very curious to see Johannesburg.

My dearly beloveds, enough for today. I must close before the tearducts open.

Loving kisses,
Your passionately loving Gerda

20th September, 1942

My dearly loved parents, I cannot write to you, so I am writing in this book.

Just imagine, on Rosh Hashanah we received a letter from you through the Red Cross! I cannot describe our joy to you. I hope it is a good sign.

Today is Erev Yom Kippur and I am just roasting a chicken. Apart from that we are having chicken soup with home-made noodles.

Today is Heini's birthday and I know that you will be thinking of us twice as much as usual.

I hope that you fast well and know that you wish us everything that is good and I also know what we are all wishing for that beast, Hitler!

Let's hope that this year will be one of fulfilment. Good Yomtov, Everything of the best,
Your Gerda

Joan

Over the years my mother and uncle made many enquiries through various channels as to the whereabouts of their parents, Samuel and Berta Mailich. Finally, in 1946 a letter was received from the South African Red Cross Society. The letter said that they were deported by the Nazis in 1942 and were not listed as having returned from any concentration camp (See photograph number 26).

However, my mother would not rest until she had more information and I remember the day in 1952 or '53 when a final letter from the Red Cross arrived to inform us that they had records to the effect that my grandparents got on a train to go to Hamburg but that they were taken off somewhere in between the two towns. They died in Auschwitz and though we did not know them we will never forget them.

In 1971 my father took ill and developed four clots on the brain. This first manifested itself in his losing his sight for about four months. Just as suddenly as he went blind his sight returned. For a while he was fine and then the clots shifted and he became childlike and no longer felt pain.

This was a very trying time for my mother as all three of her children were now living in Johannesburg and she had to cope on her own in Port Elizabeth. Without their friends I do not think that she could have managed. Every morning at six o'clock (which was the time my father automatically woke up) Bruno Kauffmann came over to get my Dad up, washed and dressed. Every evening Heinz Israel arrived to help with bathing and getting him ready for bed.

On the 9th December 1971, my beloved father, Fritz Herrmann, died.

My mother was devastated and in 1972 we finally persuaded her to go overseas with friends to find family whom she had last seen in 1936. She had kept in touch with three cousins in America and one in England, and hoped to find more family members who had survived the Holocaust.

The relatives she knew in New York arranged an evening when the three remaining cousins could all meet for the first time since the mid-thirties. It was an extremely emotional and fulfilling occasion. Freddy, Ruth and Gerda were children of first cousins and the rapport between them was, once again, immediate. Some days later they met again to introduce Gerda to their daughters and she was amazed to see how similar in looks two of the girls were to me – one older and blonder and one younger and darker! But the most amazing thing was still to come!

Their cousin, Josie Koppel, and his wife had not survived the war. They were passengers on the ill-fated 'St Louis' which sailed from Europe to Cuba with more than 600 Jews on board holding visas to live in Havana and neighbouring towns. On arrival only 36 people were admitted to Cuba and the ship had to return to Europe with its doomed cargo of passengers.

The Koppels gave their 18-month-old daughter, Judith, to a Christian family in France when they were sent back from Cuba while they tried in vain to reach safety. After the war, Judith was sent to her uncle and aunt in America and was adopted by them. The Red Cross had written to the addresses left by her parents and had also written to my parents asking if they would adopt Judith. The letter took six weeks to reach South Africa and the reply another six weeks to reach Europe. My parents waited in eager anticipation of another daughter's arrival but were bitterly disappointed when a second letter arrived telling them that Judith was already in America with closer family. Of course, this was the young woman my mother most keenly wanted to see.

When Judith walked into the reunion the family, who had not seen her for a number of years, was struck dumb by the uncanny resemblance to Gerda as a young girl!

Another strange event took place while Gerda spent time with her cousin, Lilo, in Los Angeles. A friend telephoned to give Lilo regards from Lilo's sister, Ursel, in Israel, whom Gerda was going to visit on her way back to South Africa. While speaking to her friend, Lilo suddenly remembered that the woman on the phone was somehow related to my mother from the other side of the family. The excitement when they discovered that it was my mother's long-lost cousin, Lily, whose mother was still alive and living in a retirement home in Los Angeles, was incredible. The next day the two cousins, Gerda and Lily met and my mother visited her aunt in the retirement home who tearfully mistook her for Gerda's own mother.

My mom also told them that she had named my sister Fay in memory of their daughter and sister, Fay, whom she believed to have perished in the death camps. Imagine how my mother felt when she learned that her cousin, Fay, had survived and was living in Australia! Unfortunately, they never had a chance to meet but when my sister, Fay, immigrated to Melbourne some years later, the namesakes did manage to spend some time together in Sydney.

On this first trip Gerda also met Kurt Arndt, the man to whom she had been engaged in 1935. They were immediately attracted to each other once again and when she was back home they started corresponding and making trans-Atlantic telephone calls – the wires really buzzed!

There was only one problem – Gerda could not remember why she had broken off the engagement in the first place! As she said, 'There must have been a reason!'

Kurt had escaped Germany by going to Shanghai but was arrested there and spent the war years in a Chinese Internment Camp. He always maintained that it was through my father (a man he never met) that he was able to survive those years! From my grandparents he had been able to get my mother's address in Port Elizabeth and had written to my parents telling them of the cold, the hunger and the difficulties he was experiencing in the camp. My father packed up all his European winter clothes and sent them to Kurt in Shanghai. The parcel was safely received and Kurt was able to keep warm and sell off the clothes whenever he had no money for food during the rest of his internment.

After meeting Gerda again, Kurt decided to come to South Africa for a holiday to meet the family as he was very keen to finally marry my mother. The family all liked him immediately, my children especially, as he brought them wonderful gifts from America.

We had all grown up in apartheid South Africa and though we did not have any black friends we always had a good relationship with our staff and their families as well as with our co-workers. Imagine our surprise when Kurt (who was very anti the South African government) refused to be in the same room as our black char, Selena. It turned out that he didn't like apartheid but he also didn't like black people. When asked how he handled this situation in America his answer was 'I have nothing to do with black people whatsoever, so it doesn't affect me!' That certainly gave us food for thought!

Kurt returned to America but my mother was still undecided about his offer of marriage.

He suggested she get a three-month visa to visit America to spend time with him in Seattle where he lived, in the hopes that she would enjoy it so much she would agree to stay.

We all felt that this was a good idea and off flew my globetrotting mother!

We had some letters and postcards and a few telephone calls from her but we were all rather worried as she did not sound too happy. We soon realised that she had no privacy as Kurt always added a postscript or wanted to say a few words to us on the phone so she could not ever say too much. At three o'clock one morning, our telephone rang waking us from a deep sleep. It was my mom speaking fast and in a whisper to say that she was going to leave Seattle on the first plane out and wanting to know if I would like to meet her in Europe.

Harold thought this a wonderful idea and I was incoherent with excitement as I had never had the opportunity of going abroad. However, we still did not know why Gerda was leaving Seattle.

Three weeks later I left for London – so naive were we that we arranged to meet at seven in the morning at the information desk in Heathrow airport. Neither of us realised that Heathrow had more than one terminal and many, many information desks. G'd was definitely on our side for at seven o'clock we both arrived, from different sides of the world, at the same desk!

We certainly had a lot to talk about on the bus into London. My mother finally remembered why she had broken off her engagement to Kurt – he was fanatically tidy – she was not and it nearly drove her crazy in the '30s and again in the '70s! While at his home in Seattle if she dusted and did not replace an item in the exact spot where it had been, he came and put it in its place. After a week or more of this she realised, once again, she could not go through with the marriage. There were, of course, other differences but this was the biggest stumbling block. They agreed to try for a few more weeks but in the end she felt that she had to leave.

What a magical trip around Europe she gave me! We visited seven countries in three weeks and I was allowed to choose the sights we saw. My mother had been to most of the places before but enjoyed it as much as I did as she was seeing them through new eyes.

One of the highlights for both of us was visiting Berlin, the city of her birth and youth, which she had last seen in 1936. We went to restaurants she had eaten in before, to the Kempinsky Hotel for tea as she wanted to feel what it was like to once again be welcome there and to the department stores where the family used to shop.

We were taken into East Berlin privately and spent a very emotional day with the surviving families of two of my mother's cousins. The visit laid many ghosts to rest for her and she was thrilled to be able to introduce one of her children to her family and also to be able to take me to many of the places that she had told me about while I was growing up.

This, for me was one of those days that will stay in my mind forever; it was fraught with danger and excitement! Our South African passports stated that we were not allowed into any communist country and mentioned East Germany particularly. It was a bank holiday in Germany the day we went into East Berlin and we were assured by various tour guides that we would not have any problems. We had no trouble getting through Checkpoint Charlie and into East Berlin; our car was checked and cleared and we were on our way.

My mother could not believe how things had stayed the same. Only a few new buildings were in evidence – including one on the site of her old home. When we arrived at her cousin's apartment it was exactly the same as when she had been there 36 years previously. While the cousin and his wife were in the concentration camps, a German officer and his family had been given the apartment for the duration of the war. On their release from the camps, they returned to Berlin and found that they were among the fortunate few whose homes had been well looked after by the army officer.

We had a wonderful day exploring all my mother's old haunts with me finally being able see some of the places that I had heard about since childhood.

One of the most amazing parts of that day was the sight of the image of the cross shining down from the FM tower in East Berlin. The gold non-reflective glass at the top of this tower is spherical with three panes of glass running round the observation deck which is not open to the public. From the time the sun rises in the east in the morning till it sets in the west, the slowly moving sign of the cross is visible for miles around. The population viewed it as a sign of hope!

In the late afternoon we finally bade farewell to the family and made our way back to the west where we were stopped on the German side of Checkpoint Charlie. They took our two South African passports from us and we had to wait for nearly two hours before they would let us out as we, of course, had no visas. I think my mother and I each aged nearly ten years in that time as we knew the trouble we could expect if they did not release us! It was pure luck that we were allowed through.

My mother loved life and lived it to the full. No opportunity passed her by as she wanted to experience and enjoy as much of life as possible.

She, who had been a dressmaker all her life, started working in an exclusive luggage and handbag shop on her arrival in Johannesburg in 1972. She thoroughly enjoyed this experience and stayed with them until her death in 1987.

Gerda's greatest fear was that she should become ill and be a burden to her family. She always said that she would hate to be a 'vegetable' so, with her usual flair for the dramatic, my beloved mother collapsed and died at work while serving her final customer on 10 October 1987.

The letter received after the death of Gerda Herrmann

27 December, 1977

My darlings, I hope that I will live still a few years and that I can enjoy you, and your children, but I know, that you know, what we always discussed, what I would like each of you to have.

I hope that you will always love each other, for my sake! I love you, all three – Joan, Ronny and Fay-ki very much and, therefore, I leave the money – whatever I may still have, to you three, and not to your children. Only – G'd forbid, if anything should happen to any of you, it goes, of course, to your children, and I know that Tammy, Harold and Len will understand this!

I made only one exception. In September 1977, I opened a savings account at the Standard Bank in my name, but it is intended for Tracy Broomberg (Fay's daughter), seeing that they are the least well off and Fay and Len are getting another baby, so I thought Fay should keep this for Tracy for her education or whatsoever. I know how handy money once came in for Ronnie – and how happy it made us all! Remember?

My savings account and money I have at the Permanent Building Society and this is, of course, all yours as well as my current account – I mean for you three.

You have been very lovely, loving, good children to Daddy and me and we have been very proud of you and now, after Daddy died, you are all marvellous and I know I am welcome in each of your homes! Thank you!

All my blessings, your loving Mumi

My mother then listed what each of us should have and why. How we were to divide everything – why she left something to me or Ronny and not to Fay and vice versa. She even worked out why Ronny and Tammy should not share in the bits and pieces in the sideboard for, as she put it – 'Now, it is between my daughters as Tammy will get one day – may it be a long time still – from her own mother, and I know that Tammy will understand it.'

It was all so lovingly done and one could see she had put plenty of thought into sharing out the precious things from her parents and her. However, typical of my mother, she could not resist writing to us again!

6th June, 1981

Well, I am still alive! And thanks to you, my children, I am loved and, so far, have got six lovely grandchildren! I count on Ronny to make it seven, the lucky number!

I started this letter five years ago! Hopefully, I will still live, Please G'd, a long time!

Love, love, love,

Your Mumi

EDITH'S STORY

NOTE: EDITH IS THE DAUGHTER of Joan's father's sister, Erna, and therefore Joan's first cousin.

My story is similar to that of many other Jewish children who came to Britain from Germany, Austria, Poland and the former Czechoslovakia by means of a Kindertransport.

During the infamous Kristallnacht on 9 November 1938, Jewish places of worship in Germany and Austria were set alight, Jewish properties smashed and many Jews were arrested and killed. It was then the world began to realise the horror that was to come.

Britain offered entry visas to ten thousand unaccompanied children from Germany, Austria and Czechoslovakia between the ages of three months and seventeen years. This was an act of mercy, unequalled anywhere else in the world. It was also in part to make up for their refusal to open the doors of Palestine, which could have saved a large number of European Jewry.

From 2 December 1938 to 1 September 1939, children unaccompanied by their parents came to Britain through 'Operation Kindertransports' to take refuge from Nazi persecution. They would certainly have suffered the horrors of the concentration camps and subsequent extermination if they had not been sent out of Germany. Their only crime was to be Jewish, or even half or quarter Jewish. I was half Jewish as my mother was Jewish, and my father Christian.

To process these children, a great deal of work was done by many people of many denominations. Committees were formed to establish hostels and to find homes for the children. Vast sums of money were collected as fifty pounds per child was required so they would not be a burden on the British state, and of course the children had to be maintained after their arrival. About half of the number was housed in hotels, the other half in private homes, Jewish and non-Jewish.

Most of the children lost their parents in the Holocaust and so became part of history.

It was, indeed, amazing that the Nazi authorities ever allowed these trainloads of children to leave the country on a monthly basis. The only reason I can think why they allowed this to happen was to 'cleanse' their country of Jews, and to create an 'Aryan' society. I suppose, in a way, we were lucky to escape the fate of millions of our countrymen.

The first Kindertransport left Germany in November 1938. Many Jewish parents were desperate to send their children to safety after the horrendous happenings on Kristallnacht, 9 November 1938. I personally recall being out with Annaliese, our maid, on what was probably a shopping expedition. I really adored Annaliese who was always so patient and caring. I can even remember her taking me home to visit her family on a farm. I felt so grown up sleeping in a big bed under a huge *Federbett*, an eiderdown filled with feathers, and I loved the animals on the farm.

While Annaliese and I were walking along we suddenly heard the sound of breaking glass. Quickly Annaliese pulled me away from the gathering crowds. Naturally I was curious and wanted to know what was happening but Annaliese wasted no time in taking me back home. Relatives and friends came to our house and talked furtively about what was happening to them. SS soldiers were raiding Jewish homes nightly, they reported. Houses were ransacked, furniture smashed and thrown out of windows. The Jewish men, young and old, were taken from their businesses and homes and driven away, never to return again.

Then came the night when it was our turn to have our house searched. They did not smash any furniture, although they rampaged through our house. The Jewish men from the two other flats were taken away, as was my father. Fortunately he was released some time later and we were so relieved and happy to see him again. He had undoubtedly been warned about what could happen to us all, but being a Gentile, he was allowed to come home. How upset I was, however, when two SS soldiers forced my dying grandmother out of bed. I can still see her tiny figure in a long white nightdress standing in the middle of the bedroom, hands clasped and praying. Unbeknown to me she had cancer and she passed away a few weeks later. This was the first death I had experienced in my short life and I was devastated. I adored Oma who had her own rooms in our flat. She was always the first person I went to when I came home from kindergarten and later, school.

Every thing happened very quickly after her death. I was taken shopping for new clothes, everything from underwear to a new coat and hat, even a big suitcase and a lovely little black patent case in which I could carry my little treasures. Tante Frieda, my father's sister came to visit us at this time and I recall her sitting with my mother sewing name tags on every item of my clothing, which really puzzled me. You see, I was convinced that we were going on a lovely, special holiday together, of course, with Mutti and Papa. I became quite excited but could not understand why friends came with solemn faces and gave me gifts, hugging and kissing me with tears in their eyes. It was not my birthday, so why all the presents? It all seemed so strange and bewildering. Even Annaliese, who was always bright and happy – especially when she was going out for the evening with her boyfriend, Herbert – seemed so sad and quiet.

Early one morning my father drove us to the railway station in Nordhausen. I was born and brought up in this busy town and, apart from lovely holidays in the countryside, I had not travelled very far in my seven years. I had vague recollections of visiting Leipzig but the biggest adventures had been visits to Berlin to visit Tante Lola, Oma's sister and family, and to Gütersloh in Westphalia to visit Papa's family. These visits are deeply imprinted in my mind, especially spending Hanukkah in Berlin and Christmas with my cousins Lotte and Irmgard who were older than I was and who thoroughly spoiled me.

Everything happened so quickly that I could not comprehend what was really taking place. I felt very strange. My mother came to school with me one day to see my teacher, Herr Krieghof. As my mother explained everything to him, he began to cry. I could not believe my eyes. A teacher crying, that was something I had never seen before. I was very fond of this teacher who had twinkling eyes behind spectacles and rosy cheeks rather like the composer Schubert, I realised in later years.

That last drive to the railway station was to be my farewell to Nordhausen. My father, Hermann Twelkemeier, did not come with us on the train to Hanover but that did not worry me. He was a man with a business to run and I thought he would follow us later. I still believed this was a big adventure, like going on a special holiday. My mother had tried I'm sure, to explain to me that we were to be separated for a time but that she would soon be following. She had, I discovered many years later, been planning to come to Britain to work as a domestic servant. Sadly her plan did not come to fruition.

In Hanover we visited friends who had a lovely little boy with whom I played and we had our photograph taken together. Then in the evening my mother took me to the railway station and I had a strange foreboding that things were not as I had expected. She kissed and hugged me quickly, put me on the train and to my horror and disbelief did not climb in with me. In fact, this train was packed with what seemed to be hundreds of children all of different ages. Clutching my little case I stood petrified and bewildered. What was happening? Where was Mutti? Why was I left alone for the first time in my life surrounded by so many children that I could not even get near a window to look for Mutti? Suddenly the train jerked forward and I remember shouting at the top of my voice, 'Mutti! Mutti!' Somebody, a boy I think, lifted me up so I could look out of the window. I saw her standing on the platform, her lovely big eyes frantically looking for me, but she did not see me. That was the last time I saw my beloved Mutti.

Afterwards I sat numb and silent in an overcrowded train and for the first time in my life I was really afraid. Why was I alone on this train? Where was I going? No answers came because I never uttered these questions aloud, but they were whirling round in my mind. We seemed to travel for hours until we reached the sea. In the darkness I could discern the shape of a huge ship. We had arrived at the Hook of Holland and would be sailing to Harwich in England.

Looking back it seems that most of that terrible journey took place in darkness. We had left our parents on a dark evening, the train and bus trips were in the dark and we also sailed during the night. This was my first glimpse of the sea and I had certainly never been on a big boat before. The girl with whom I shared a cabin was several years older than myself and was very seasick during the night. I helped her and she took my lower berth while I scrambled up onto the upper one.

When we disembarked more train and bus trips awaited us until we finally arrived in London. Here we were dispatched to a huge hall where we were fed. All I can remember of that meal was the fact that I was given a cup of drinking chocolate which I knocked over. The sight of the brown liquid running down the centre of the white tablecloth made me cry for the first time since I had left my mother.

Today I often think of the anguish she and the other Jewish parents must have endured sending their children on a Kindertransport. I was an only and much loved child and suddenly, like a fledging, I had been cast out of a warm nest. We were, of course, being sent to safety. Many of these brave parents, including my mother, were to perish in Auschwitz or other concentration camps.

After a short period in London, I do not recall how long, yet more bus and train trips lay ahead of us. Everyone was talking so fast and in a very strange language. People kept looking at the labels on our clothes to see our names. Several fortunate children were met by relatives and taken away by them. I knew nobody and the groups we travelled with continued to change. I must have slept on the last train journey because it again took place at night. When we got off the train we were met by yet another group of people as well as reporters and photographers and our picture appeared in the Edinburgh *Evening News*. I still have an enlarged copy of the photograph today.

This photograph was seen by a very wonderful Christian couple who, having lost their own baby, decided to apply to the Scottish Christian Council for Refugees for a Jewish child. They saw me, the youngest child, standing at the front of the group, still clutching my little black case and holding the hand of a boy who looked a little older than me. I have no recollection of having even spoken to him and, believe it or not, I was actually smiling as I looked at the camera. Nancy and Gavin Forrester decided to ask for me as they felt they wanted me. They immediately set the wheels in motion while we were being driven to an orphanage in Selkirk in the Borders region of Scotland.

We all disliked this place on sight, and hated the dormitories where we heard mice scrabbling about behind the skirting boards. The food was so unlike anything we were accustomed to but the members of staff were very kind to us.

I shall never forget the first time I saw Nancy and Gavin. The matron took me to a room where they were waiting. They immediately stood up and smiled at me. We could not communicate, of course, because they did not speak German and I spoke no English. I felt then, for the first time since leaving Germany that here were two people whom I could trust. Would they take me with them? Where did they live? Who were they? All these questions buzzed around in my mind but it was some time later before I was finally able to join them.

I believe I was the first child in that group to find a home and it was a long time, in fact 50 years, before I saw any of the other children again. The first one was, to my amazement, the boy whose hand I had been holding in the newspaper photograph. The other two were the sisters standing on either side of us. It was an emotional reunion.

There were several complications and misunderstandings before I was finally delivered into the care of Nancy and Gavin Forrester. Other people were also keen to take me into their care, but Gavin, being a very astute and determined gentleman, finally 'won the day'.

Matron took me by train to Edinburgh and my spirits lifted when I recognised Nancy and Gavin waiting for me at the station. Again we could only smile at one another but they took me by the hand and led me to another platform to catch a train to Kirkcaldy. This seemingly endless journey was soon to be over. I had no idea where I was or where I was going but for the first time since leaving home I felt no fear.

We walked the short distance from the station to the bank house. Gavin was the manager and Nancy and he lived in the flat above the bank. As Gavin opened the front door I heard the sound of scurrying feet and to my surprise and joy, a beautiful brown and white cocker spaniel jumped all over me, licking my face and knees. Gavin and Nancy tried to quieten Eddy, but he and I were too busy getting acquainted to take notice of them. We were both so excited. Here was *somebody* I could communicate with at last. Afterwards Nancy told me that they had been very worried in case I was frightened of dogs.

From that moment on, Eddy refused to leave my side. He even tried to follow me into the bathroom and wanted to jump onto the bed at night to sleep with me. He became very protective of me and whined when I left him for even a short time.

When I used to practise the piano, I had to play scales and Eddy would 'howl in key', much to the consternation of the staff downstairs in the bank. Dad, as I learned to call Gavin eventually, often had to phone Mum and ask her to stop me playing.

The language barrier had to be overcome. I kept asking for Annaliese and *meine Puppe*. Nobody had remembered to pack my favourite doll in the last minute rush. Perhaps she was too big to pack. Anyhow, she was soon replaced by a beautiful, blue-eyed doll which Mum and Dad bought for me. I was so delighted to hold this lovely doll with her blue hat, dress and little white shoes.

A German teacher, who was to become a life-long friend, came to interpret for our family. Sign language also worked wonders. Mum panicked on one occasion when she served tomato soup. I had never seen red soup before and stupidly began to cry. However, I had been trained to eat everything which was put before me, so there were few dietary problems. In Germany I had a set of dishes on which nursery rhymes were painted and I was always very keen to discover the rhyme on the bottom of the plate.

It was decided that I should enrol at the local primary school as soon as possible. The infant mistress there was a personal friend of Mum and Dad's and she suggested that I should work along with the infants until I gained enough knowledge of English. Every morning the bell would ring at the bank house and when we opened the door a little group of children would chorus 'We've come to take Edith to school'. Dutifully and somewhat shyly I would clasp their hands and off we would trot the short distance to school.

Within six weeks, I am told, I began to forget my German and spoke English, with an accent, but at least with more confidence. I was then transferred into a class of children of my own age and later was even allowed to skip a class because of the good progress I had made. I loved reading and was a regular visitor to the local library, and still am today.

At the age of twelve I passed the examination to transfer to the high school, where I stayed for six years, specialising in French, German, English and Latin. When I left school I took and passed my final piano exam as well as a crash course in shorthand and typewriting, which have stood me in good stead over the years. However, I made the decision not to go to university, which was a great disappointment to Mum and Dad.

My teenage years were not very happy ones because during this period I learned about the atrocities committed by the Nazis. I also made a personal discovery about the fate of my mother during this time. I was about 14 years old when, quite by accident, I discovered what had happened to my beloved mother Erna. I remember coming home from high school for lunch as usual and going to fetch some papers from the writing bureau. A large envelope fell out and I picked it up. Suddenly I realised it contained reports from my mother's cousin, Kurt Herrmann, who had escaped from a concentration camp and gone to America. He had served as a GI in Germany and had been sent to the concentration camps to file reports.

In trepidation I opened the envelope and started to read the about the horrors of what had been discovered at the liberation of these camps, especially Auschwitz and Therensienstadt, where my mother, Kurt's parents and his grandmother perished.

I heard someone screaming and only realised that it was my own voice when Mum came running in to see what was wrong. I heard her moaning 'Oh no! Oh no!' They were keeping the papers from me until I was older and able to cope with the enormity of such horror, anguish and pain. She just held me in her arms and tried to comfort me. I grew up overnight. I was in a state of shock for many months, having read reports about the conditions in the concentration camps. We saw news-reels of the horrors and I had nightmares after seeing the dead bodies and emaciated bodies of survivors.

It was a very long time before I was able to laugh, even smile again. Mum and Dad were so loving and patient with me. My school friends must have wondered what had happened to me but I could not discuss it with anyone. I locked the pain deep in my heart, vowed I would never go back to Germany and would have nothing to do with anybody or anything from Germany. I was filled with loathing and disgust. How could six million lives have been snuffed out so cruelly and with pre-meditation?

Even now, after so many years, it is very difficult to talk or to write about my feelings. I am often asked to give my testimony in Christian churches, clubs, and schools. I have appeared twice on television with other refugees who came to Britain on a Kindertransport. Each time I am left drained and saddened but always try to present my story in a sincere, simple way without sentimentality. After all, I was one of the fortunate children to escape the clutches of Hitler's extermination machine.

I often think of the anguish of my own parents who lost their only child. My mother had intended to follow me to Britain but, of course, that did not materialise. Hope died for so many Jewish people and my story is not as sad as those of so many others whose entire families died in con-centration camps.

Eventually I did go to university to study for a degree in German and French, having worked as a civil servant for two years. Never once did Mum and Dad try to influence me in my decisions. I know, neverthe-less, that they were delighted when I decided to go to university. They paid the fees and all my allowances, which could not have been easy, as bankers' salaries were quite modest.

I decided to train as a social worker after I obtained my degree. I most certainly did not want to teach. However, I was advised by one of my favourite teachers to go to teacher training college for a year as she thought I would make a good teacher. When I stepped into a classroom at my first teaching practice session I knew that this was the profession for me. I enjoyed working with children and spent thirty-one years of my life doing just that. If I had my life over again I believe I would do the same. I am still in contact with many of my students.

I progressed through the ranks from ordinary class teacher to assistant teacher, principal teacher, lady advisor to female students and finally assistant rector in charge of the guidance of all students aged between 15 and 18. During these years I went back to Germany on visits and to take part in courses for teachers. At first my feelings of hatred were very strong, especially towards people of a certain age who might have been involved in military activities. I was troubled by these feelings, having been brought up in a loving, Christian environment, but I was unable to rid myself of them.

During the war years and the post-war era I had to be careful not to disclose my German/Jewish background. Deep down, however, I longed to research the beliefs and traditions of my people, the Jews. The opportunity to do so came much later, after the deaths of Mum and Dad. Dad passed away very suddenly after a massive heart attack in 1977 and Mum a little more than two years later, also after an unexpected heart attack. I was deeply saddened by their passing and found myself unable to pray or go to church. My one desire was to go to Israel. Without telling anyone about my intentions I made an appointment to see my doctor about the necessary vaccinations and arranged my itinerary. I chose a Jewish led tour and visited all the Jewish places of interest. The two places high on my list were, of course, the Western or Wailing Wall and the Yad Vashem Holocaust Memorial.

Everything impressed me deeply and within myself I confessed to G'd that I wanted to embrace Judaism as my mother and her relatives knew and loved it. G'd, however, had other plans for me. One evening as we stood on the banks of the River Jordan it was growing dark and the Holy Spirit filled me with warmth from head to toe, telling me to be baptised. If somebody had offered to baptise me there and then in the waters of the River Jordan I would gladly have done so!

The following day our guide Zvi took us to Yad Vashem. Here part of me died when I saw the Eternal Flame burning for the six million victims of the Holocaust, and the horrific photographs in the Museum. It became very clear to me that I could have been one of the million Jewish children who perished in the camps. But for the grace of G'd and the Kindertransport I might never have survived.

After the visit the bus took us back to town and I went up to my hotel room where I wept bitter tears, praying to G'd for guidance and peace of mind. Eventually I fell asleep and woke much later. It was dark and I suddenly felt a tremendous peace, a Shalom that has never left me in spite of many disappointments and some frustrations. I knew I had been cleansed of all hatred and bitterness.

When I returned home I saw the minister of the Baptist Church and told him my whole story. My baptism was a most moving and exhilarating experience. Helen, my best friend, stood up with me and I prayed aloud before I entered the waters of baptism. The words asking for G'd's forgiveness for all the hatred I had felt towards all Germans came involuntarily. As I prayed, once again my whole body was suffused with a wonderful warmth and peace.

I knew that I now had the joy of both worlds. I love the Jewish festivals, which I celebrate throughout the year, just as my own dearest mother, Erna Herrmann, did and as my other Jewish relatives still do today. I pray for all my fellow Jews throughout the world, but especially in Israel which is fighting for its very survival. I believe G'd has a purpose for this land of ours. No amount of infighting among politicians or military personnel will decide its fate. It is in the hands of G'd Almighty.

I was a very confused person for several years but the turning point came to me after that visit to the Yad Vashem Holocaust Museum. There the search for my true identity came to an end. At long last I realised that I had shut the door on my past and had hidden and ignored my inner self. I also knew that I would never find peace and true happiness unless I accepted myself for what I was: Jewish by race and very proud of it, German by birth and British by choice, also very proud of it, but above all a child of G'd.

One of the 'Kinder', Vera Gissing, a Czech by birth, has written a very moving account of her experiences. Like me, she came to a stage in her life when she was confused about her own identity. She was Jewish, born a Czech, yet brought up in Britain, so she went back to Prague, thinking she might settle in her native land. One day she visited a Holocaust museum in Prague and she wrote a book called *Pearls of Childhood* (St. Edmundsbury Press). In it she says 'This was a turning point in my life, because it was there, in that small museum of the Holocaust, that my search for my identity ended. I realised at long last that by shutting out the past I had closed the door on my inner self and that I would never find peace and true happiness unless I accepted myself for what I was: Jewish by race, Czech by birth and British by choice.'

I echo Vera's thoughts and words – I am Jewish by race and very proud of it, German by birth and British by choice. Most importantly, however, I am a child of G'd and by His mercy I was selected to live.

Note: The following letter was received by Willi Herrmann, Edith's uncle, in Cali, Colombia, after the war and has been translated into

English – it has not been corrected. It refers to Erna and Hermann Twelkemeier (Edith's parents) and Ella and Max Baruch. Max and Ella got divorced and Erna later married Max Baruch. Herman and Ella were Christians while Erna and Max were Jewish. While we are not certain of what happened to my father, Hermann Twelkemeier, we do know that he and my mother divorced.

1st September, 1947

From Mrs Ella Ankermann, Berlin, Germany

My dear Mr Herrmann!

Only today I can get in touch with you, since I was totally bombed out a day before the Russians occupied our city. I lost everything I owned; it went up in flames including my address book. A few days ago I received your address from Mrs Griessmayer in Munich; Mr Hermann Twelkemeier in Nordhausen was not able to provide it for me.

I am getting in touch with you in the name of the former Mrs Erna Twelkemeier, later Mrs Baruch. She got married for the second time on November 20, 1941, to Mr Max Baruch, who was my first husband. She had asked me to send to you her very last greetings from your niece. Erna and her husband have perished; Max was shipped to Jawischowitz, which was a sub-camp from Auschwitz. I once received news from him, but my letters were never answered. Before their deportation I was in touch with both of them and I tried my best to help them in their terrible situation by providing them with food articles and also money. We were in the middle of a war and did not get much doled out either, but I felt happy that I was able to help them, even it if meant a sacrifice to me.

Both had hoped to the very end even after the arrest by the Gestapo, that thanks to Erna's earlier marriage (to Hermann Twelkemeier) they would be protected from deportation because he was Christian. But no such luck! The mother of Max Baruch was also arrested four weeks later at her place of work. We tried our best to get them liberated, but again no such luck! Both husband and wife got separated and were put into special assembly camps in Berlin, but somehow they could stay in touch with each other through messengers.

Erna continued to go to work at her place of work and I kept in touch with her continuously. On February 2nd she called me by phone and asked me to meet her. She told me then, she had received a message from her husband, she should prepare herself for deportation. She should ask me for some money and some food for the trip. I did give her some money and some food and some pieces of jewellery, which might come in handy, who knows what the situation might be. Later on I heard that both of them were deported and from Max the news from Jawischowitz and following this, nothing ever. In my letters I always inquired about Erna's whereabouts, but I never received an answer again.

Erna requested that I should get in touch with you and your brother, to notify you all what had taken place and what became of Erna. She also asked me to take care of little Edith, in case she ever needed any help. There still existed the possibility that Hermann Twelkemeier might be called to duty in the army! Mr Twelkemeier notified me though, that Edith is feeling very well and well taken care of by her 'adopted parents'. I, therefore, did not get in touch with Edith to cause any unrest; after all she should forget this time period. Recently I went to Nordhausen, which by the way does not look badly bombed. Mr Twelkemeier got married again to a 20-year-old young lady, on August 23, 1947.

You used to live in Gotha, which is also not badly damaged from the bombings. Berlin got terribly damaged; do you know the city? Good for those that do not have to live in Germany any longer. Our life consists of being hungry, to freeze and in winter to sit in the dark. We are short of clothes to wear, especially warm ones. Those that were bombed out have to suffer especially hard. Our future does not look rosy at all and will not change in the near future either. Our situation is one of desolation, and if I could leave tomorrow, I would be willing to emigrate to anywhere. I have given up hope that our dear ones will ever return from the horrible places they were condemned to.

My husband and I separated in July 1941. He had an affidavit to emigrate to a safe country and believed we could save certain things for him and for me if we divorced before his emigration. All our money, etc. was in my husband's name and if we divorced, it would be put into my name and I would then be able to support myself. Suddenly the Gestapo entered the picture and threatened to force us to divorce. They were interested in our real estate for one of the Party's bigwigs! Since we were to evacuate our quarters and did not know what to do with our furniture and where to store it, my husband filed for divorce so that everything could be put into my name. Erna and Max got married on the 29th November 1941 and they always thought they would escape the deportation thanks to Erna's former marriage to Hermann Twelkemeier who was Christian. We unfortunately did not have any children; then things would be been different, I suppose.

How do you feel living in Cali, Colombia? Have you gotten assimilated and are you Colombian citizen already?

I think very often of both of them, Max and Erna. I wished they had a better destiny. I liked your niece very much and she liked me too and she knew that I would do everything for both of them what I could possibly have done even to great sacrifice to myself.

Write to me sometimes.

With friendly greetings,
Frau Ella Ankermann

1

2

7

8

9

10

11

14.8.40.
Mamilein - Süßbab - ...
war ich wieder beim Arzt
alle 4 Wochen, ...

13

14

15

16

17

18

19

20

21

22

23

18. 11. 40.

Geliebte goldene Mutti,

Baby ist endlich da! Und

Ihr habt eine Enkeltochter!

Wir sind selig! Vorabend

den 16. 11. mittags 1 30ʰ

Kam das kleine Luder

~~Freitag~~ Vorabend morgen um 6³⁰

hat Fritz mich eingeholt

und sah schon stark

24

25

26

CENTRAL EXECUTIVE COMMITTEE

SENTRALE UITVOERENDE KOMITEE

THE SOUTH AFRICAN
DIE SUID-ÁFRIKAANSE

RED CROSS SOCIETY
ROOIKRUISVERENIGING

OFFICES: HIS MAJESTY'S BUILDING, ELOFF STREET, JOHANNESBURG, SOUTH AFRICA
KANTORE: HIS MAJESTY'S-GEBOU, ELOFFSTRAAT, JOHANNESBURG, SUID-AFRIKA
TELEGRAMS "REDCROSS." TELEGRAMME   P.O. BOX 8726 POSBUS   TELEPHONES 33-3421/2/3/4 TELEFONE

PRESIDENT:—DIE REGTER—THE HON. JUSTICE O. D. SCHREINER.
HON. NATIONAL TREASURER ERE NASIONALE TESOURIER W. PATRICK JONES, ESQ.

ALL COMMUNICATIONS TO BE ADDRESSED
TO THE GENERAL SECRETARY
AND NOT TO INDIVIDUALS

| IN REPLY PLEASE QUOTE |
| WR/19398. |
| IN ANTWOORD MELD ASSEBLIEF |

ALLE KORRESPONDENSIE MOET AAN DIE
ALGEMENE SEKRETARIS GERIG WORD
EN NIE AAN INDIVIDUELE PERSONE NIE.

4th February 1946.

Mrs. G.Herrmann,
4,Monaco Flats,
Cuyler Street,
PORT ELIZABETH.

Dear Mrs. Herrmann,

With reference to your enquiry for news of

SAMUEL MAILICH.

we have now received the following communication from the Search
Bureau Control Commission:

Samuel and Bert Mailich are reported to have been deported
by the Nazis about 1942.
Their names do not appear on the lists of Jews who have
returned to Berlin from concentration camps.

As lists of persons who have returned to Berlin will not
be complete until April at the earliest, the names have been
recorded and further investigations will be made in due course.

We hope to have more heartening news for you at a later
date, and assuring you of our willing assistance at all times.

Yours sincerely,

Stella Cohen

FOR: GENERAL SECRETARY. J.M.

WR/547Z.

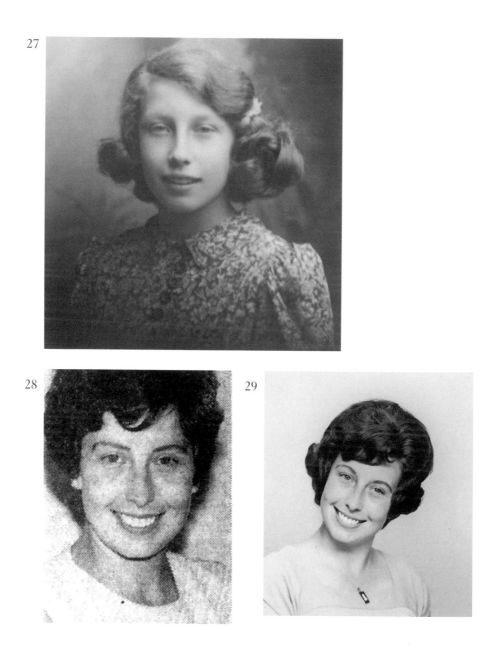

30

31

32

33

34

35

36

KURT'S STORY

Dedicated to Robert, Joshua and Jonathan

Introduction

MY NAME IS KURT J. HERRMANN, the only son of Harry and Rosel Herrmann, nee Moses. My father Harry had three brothers and one sister. Theodor and his wife Else Herrmann, nee Braumann; Willi and Claire Herrmann, nee Braumann.
You will notice that the two brothers married two sisters. Then there was Max Herrmann, who died early in his life and is buried in the Jewish cemetery in the city of Nordhausen, Germany. Last but not least were Joseph and Margarete Frank, nee Herrmann, the only girl in the family. All four siblings were born in the city of Nordhausen, one of those thousand-year-old towns at the southern foot of the Harz Mountains in central Germany.

Theodor and Else Herrmann had two sons, Walter and Fritz and one daughter, Erna. Fritz married Gerda Mailich after emigrating to South Africa. Fritz Herrmann was my first cousin.

Willi and Claire Herrmann had three daughters, Edith, Ilse and Lieselotte.

Joseph Frank (Seppi) and Margarete Frank had one son, Rudi and one daughter, Charlotte.

Our grandparents were Julius and Rosalie Herrmann, Rosalie was born in Nordhausen in 1843 and we can trace her ancestors back to 1767. Julius Herrmann was born in Goslar on the north rim of the Harz Mountains in 1839. In about 1866 he moved to Nordhausen, where he met Rosalie. We can trace his ancestors back to 1762. Both Julius and Rosalie are buried in the Jewish Cemetery in Nordhausen.

By now you have read the stories of Fritz and Gerda Herrmann and also of Erna's (Fritz's sister) daughter Edith Forrester. Remember, it happened over 65 years ago and I am glad I have put it down on paper.

The Nazi jolt

The serenity and tranquillity of the comfortable life in Nordhausen, as well as elsewhere in Germany, was jolted by the take-over of the government by the Nazis in 1933. From the very beginning all their actions were directed against the Jews of Germany. At the start people believed that in due course things would settle down and life would return to some semblance of normality.

We Jews were to find out differently; the Nazi's racist policies were turned into decrees implemented by the government. Each year the situation worsened and the only solution to this problem seemed to be to leave Germany for good. The German government actively encouraged Jews to emigrate, as long as they left everything they owned behind in Germany. You were allowed to leave with RM10.00 and under those conditions you were expected to start anew in a foreign country whose language you did not speak.

There were approximately 500 000 Jews living in Germany; 375 000 were able to emigrate; 125 000 perished in the Holocaust that followed during World War II. These pages will tell you the story of how some of the Herrmann family were influenced by Nazi persecution and atrocities.

In 1938 I lost my job with Becker Bros in Chemnitz as this company, like so many others, was cleansed of Jewish personnel. The only option left for me to do was to emigrate somewhere in this world. Fortunately we had a well-to-do relative in New York and he had his heart in the right place and he sent me an affidavit saying that he would support me in the United States and that I would not be a burden on the country. I registered with the American consulate in Berlin for an application for emigration and I received a number which some day would be called up. If I was still interested when my number came up, I could then file the necessary papers for immigration.

The year was late 1938.

Recent actions by the Gestapo had made all of us feel uneasy and we had to consider spending the period waiting for our visas to come through in an interim country. Cuba was a popular choice and many people had taken advantage of her generous conditions.

It was hard to come by steamship passage to Cuba as there were not many ships leaving for that part of the world. Fortunately I was able to book passage on the 'Orinoco'; if I received my US visa in the meantime, I could always cancel my ticket. There were plenty of other people who would be willing to take it up.

Early in November 1938 Cuba changed her visa requirements – one now had to have US$5 000 deposited in a Cuban bank or else no visa would be issued. Since I had no foreign money abroad, using Cuba as an interim country was no longer an option.

My father and I left Nordhausen on 9 November 1938 for Leipzig where my father was to pay a visit to his sister Grete (Margarete Frank) and I was to return my ticket on the 'Orinoco'. My father remained in Leipzig intending to stay for a few days, while I returned to Nordhausen. Upon arriving home, I went to bed early.

At two o'clock in the morning, there was a loud knock on our apartment door. An elderly policeman stood outside and asked us to get dressed and come downstairs with him. 'Dress warmly,' he said, 'and lock your apartment door well.'

I heard a lot of commotion downstairs in the street, and I could not resist taking a quick look out of our front window. I could not see what was actually taking place, but I noticed a huge red glow over the city, which meant that there was a major fire burning.

We followed the policeman downstairs. A car driven by two storm troopers pulled up at the kerb, and the elderly policeman asked us to get into the back of the vehicle. My grandmother, my mother and I obeyed, and then we were taken for a 'sightseeing trip' through the city. The inner city was being destroyed, stores' large display windows had been smashed, their contents looted or thrown into the street. Furniture, mattresses, utensils and bedding had been thrown out of apartments and broken glass lay everywhere! Cars containing other Jewish families were cruising up and down the main streets of our city. Our storm troopers were yelling at the tops of their voices, 'Death to the Jews' or their favourite songs like 'When Jewish blood drips off our knives . . .' and other songs. This madness seemed incomprehensible!

We now turned into a street called the Pferdemarkt, where the fiery-red sky gave us a hint of what they had done to our synagogue. We stopped at the fiercely burning house of worship and they made us watch as it burned to the ground. Our congregational building next to the synagogue was a total wreck too.

Leaving this scene of horror we were treated to more destruction, street by street. When was this nightmare going to end? Eventually they dropped us off at an old assembly hall called the Siechhof. As we arrived there, we saw other Jewish families who had been dumped there before us and gradually the large room filled to capacity. The outside of the building was guarded by police and Gestapo agents, and what our fate would be, only G'd would know.

We spent the whole night there, all family members, regardless of age. At dawn they dismissed all the women, the very old and the very young, and permitted them to go back to their homes and apartments. All the men between the ages of 12 and 70 were kept in protective custody. Later on in the morning two large buses pulled up and we all had to board them and we were shipped off to destination unknown.

After a while it became obvious that we were heading for the KZ Buchenwald, one of the most notorious camps inside Germany. After several hours of travelling we arrived at the main gate of Buchenwald, across the arch of the gate large letters said 'Work makes you free'. The camp's storm troopers were expecting us and they chased us out of the buses through the main gate onto the assembly square where we had to line up. Little did we know that we were going to stand there for the rest of the day. To our left a large contingent was already standing in line, they had all been very badly beaten and were all bloody. Someone recognized them as the Jews of the city of Erfurt. All day long buses rolled in from various cities throughout Germany, depositing their Jewish citizens. I noticed when the Jews from Hildesheim or from Chemnitz arrived, but none of them had been mistreated as badly as the ones from Erfurt. As we heard later, Erfurt had the distinction of being the city treated the worst of all.

Lining up on the assembly square became a very painful experience. It was particularly bad for the elderly who could not stand on their feet for very long, and dropped left and right. When we were permitted to sit down for a while it too became painful since we were not allowed to stand up and stretch or else we would be mown down with machine guns from the nearby watchtowers. The greatest pain, however, was created by our own bodies. We all had a great urgency to relieve ourselves, and we had nowhere to go but into our own clothes. We hoped that it would dry quickly and the discomfort would not last. This, by the way, was the Gestapo's method of creating a 'stinking Jew'.

Although we had nothing to eat all day long, we were not hungry, we all felt too miserable and degraded. Food was the last thing on our minds. Some time during the day they shaved off our hair and made us look awkward. We were most uncomfortable and also cold; winter starts early in the Thuringia woods.

In the late afternoon work commandos returned from their assignments and joined the ranks on the assembly square. We were now to witness a new spectacle, the penalty for those who had violated camp rules or who were guilty of other infractions. Their names were called out and the poor victim had to step out of rank and the storm troop commander sentenced him to a number of lashes, administered at once. There were no penalties under twenty-five lashes. They strapped the poor fellow onto a wooden block, lowered his pants and administered the lashes with a leather whip. Animal-like screams came from the poor victim and eventually turned into moans. After twelve to fifteen lashes, there were no more sounds. When the penalty was paid, the person was dragged away to the infirmary. Immediately thereafter the next victim was strapped in, and the process repeated itself until all cases were taken care of. What were the crimes they had committed? Perhaps they failed to salute an officer or they did not march at double-time when they were supposed to. Major crimes, like trying to escape, or resisting a storm trooper were punishable by death, usually by hanging. Their bodies would be left hanging for some time to serve as a deterrent for others.

The camp was administered by the black-uniformed storm troopers and the prisoners were under the immediate command of the so-called *Kapos* who were hardened criminals who could 'redeem' themselves at Buchenwald instead of lingering in jail. Some of these 'toughs' were murderers and they did not care if any of the prisoners died or not. There were always new batches of prisoners arriving in the camp and they wouldn't run short of slave labour.

Finally in the evening we were fed and assigned to our respective barracks which had very large outdoor latrine facilities. This seemed to be the greatest luxury of all; finally we could relieve ourselves after a whole day's urgency.

The barracks consisted of five-tiered shelves, and you crawled into one of these spaces and shared it with four other people. If one person turned over in his sleep during the night, the other four had to follow suit. The older men got the lower spaces, and the young guys had to climb to the very top.

Lying in my shelf-space I reflected on what the last 24 hours had meant for us all; our future looked grim and dark indeed. Was there any chance left to emigrate to America at all? Maybe all foreign nations would make it easier for us to emigrate after what had happened within the last 24 hours. Or was this just wishful thinking? Totally exhausted, I fell asleep without a blanket or mattress. During the night I woke up to screams; people were having nightmares. There were no lights in the barracks during the night-time. People were huddling in little groups and discussing their plight in the darkness; others were saying their prayers.

The next day our outlook was not any rosier. They fed us in the morning and then we lined up on the assembly square. The Gestapo had not been able to resist arresting a totally feeble-minded person known as Ernst. He lived in a mental institute. Nevertheless they shipped him with us to KZ Buchenwald. The guards had also found out about this fellow and were having their fun with him. They put him in charge of our group and we had to follow his commands! The result was total havoc, until one large SS man grabbed him by his necktie, lifted him up and began to twirl him in one direction until he went blue in the face. He then let him un-twirl and twirled him in the other direction until the same thing happened. This game went on and on, until one of our physicians was called to the infirmary to identify the body of Ernst.

The father of the cantor of our synagogue was a very learned and intelligent man, but his answers were at times a bit snappy. The guards did not like this at all and they strung him up on a large tree. They tied his hands behind his back in order to create maximum pain. The pain must have been so great that his mind snapped and several hours later they took down his lifeless body. His son had witnessed his father's suffering. He could not face up to all this brutality and that same evening he committed suicide by jumping into the open-air latrine, where he suffocated. During the next night others committed suicide by jumping into and onto the electric barbed wire surrounding the camp. The guards left their bodies dangling on the fence for all to see. This was one way to finish it all.

One hopeful sign up until this point was the fact that we were not made to change into camp clothing, but were permitted to wear our street attire.

There was a postal embargo and nobody was allowed to send out any mail, nor were we allowed to receive any type of mail. Later on the embargo was lifted and I requested more warm clothing from my mother. In no time I received a package from Nordhausen, containing warm clothing including long underwear and heavy ski socks. Day by day it got nastier in the Thuringia woods; the weather matched the atmosphere at KZ Buchenwald.

The food was edible, although I would not recommend it. We were fed twice a day, but on Sunday there was no food at all. Instead the camp orchestra played all day long!

One day they fed us whale meat; it tasted okay but we all got a violent case of diarrhoea. The camp command locked us into our barracks and nobody was allowed to go outside to the latrine. The mess and stench in our barrack was indescribable and is better left to your own imagination.

After two weeks of incarceration in Buchenwald, suddenly there was an announcement over the loudspeaker system: 'All those who have tickets to leave the country should report to camp headquarters immediately.' I had to make a very difficult decision: should I bluff my way out of Buchenwald and face the consequences if my trick was discovered? As coincidence would have it, I was still wearing the same suit that I had worn on my trip to Leipzig. In one of the pockets I found a receipt from the travel agency which stated that I had booked passage on the 'Orinoco' to Havana, Cuba. Nobody knew that I had returned the ticket, except the travel agency, and I had my doubts that the Nazis would get in touch with the agency.

My decision then was to go to headquarters and ask for my release from KZ Buchenwald. To my surprise, they treated us humanely at the camp headquarters and their reply to my request was that they had to check with our local Gestapo first! The local Gestapo did not know that I had cancelled my trip to Cuba and therefore my chances of being released from Buchenwald were pretty good. My number one aim was to get out of Buchenwald and number two, to leave the country as soon as I possibly could.

Exactly three weeks after my arrest, my name was called out from a list of prisoners to be discharged from KZ Buchenwald. We were to assemble at a separate location where we received an orientation lesson regarding our future. We were not to talk to anybody about KZ Buchenwald. If we were caught doing so, we would find ourselves right back where we were. We were to travel only in third-class coaches on the trains and eat at third-class railway dining halls. We were declared to be 'free game'. Anybody who beat us up or even killed us would not be prosecuted. Our lives, or any Jewish life, were not worth 'one Pfennig'!

And with that they told us to run off into the woods to find our way home. To make us run a bit faster, they fired several rounds from machine guns and rifles after us. Oskar Stiebel from Eisenach, a distant relative of ours, was running next to me and was grazed on his hand by one of the stray bullets. Luckily it was not a serious injury and he kept on running to get far enough from camp.

Our next worry was to find a public telephone to call a taxi that would drive us to the railway station. We eventually found a phone in a restaurant in a small village nearby. A taxi took us to the Weimar railway station and I took the train to Erfurt and on to Nordhausen. In Erfurt I made a quick phone call home to tell them of my arrival and to prepare a hot bath for me. There was great joy when my family saw me stepping into the apartment, hale and healthy, but without any hair. Never was a hot bath as wonderful as this one; and never did I need a bath as urgently as I did then!

While having a bite to eat, my parents brought me up to date on what had taken place in the previous three weeks. My mother and grandmother returned to our apartment early in the morning on 10 November and found it undamaged and the front door locked, the same way we had left it when we were arrested. The fact that the *Allgemeine Zeitung* had their offices downstairs in the building might have contributed to us being left alone. The *Allgemeine Zeitung* was the official Nazi publication in Nordhausen.

My father stayed with his sister Grete and her husband Seppi in Leipzig and was not molested. Upon the insistence of the Gestapo in Nordhausen, my father had to return and was promptly arrested and put into the city jail. Luckily enough he was not shipped to KZ Buchenwald.

My mother was able to contact Mr Hagen, our former neighbour, who worked for the criminal police department in Nordhausen and asked him if he could help my father. He promptly did. He went to the jail, unlocked the door of my father's cell and sent my father home. My father was incarcerated for less than 24 hours. While in jail my father listened to the rehearsals of the Christmas music in the nearby Market Church, located right behind the jail cells.

They told me of the tragedy that befell Mrs Singer. The Gestapo notified her that her husband had died in Buchenwald but then they came back two hours later to notify her that a mistake had been made. Her husband had not died, but her son had. A couple of hours later the Gestapo came back to her again to tell her that both men were dead. The poor, poor woman had lost everyone.

Those of us that were released from KZ Buchenwald were required to report to our local Gestapo headquarters within 24 hours. In the beginning we had to report to the Gestapo every day, later on it was altered to every other day and eventually to once a week. Any trip outside the city had to be approved by the Gestapo first.

Our main aim was to leave Germany as quickly as possible, but to my consternation all foreign countries closed their doors to us after the happenings of 10 November. If it was difficult to get a visa before, it was doubly so now! We expected foreign countries to open their doors to us; instead they shut their doors in our faces! Ten per cent of all Jews caught in the 'net' became victims of Nazi atrocities. The world stood by and let it happen. Germany had 500 000 Jewish citizens and no foreign country cared enough to save them from Nazi atrocities.

The Gestapo pressurised us to leave for abroad as soon as possible, always threatening, 'We can put you back into Buchenwald if you do not comply.'

Rumour had it that one should not try the consulates in Berlin but rather rely on a chance for an entry visa at consulates located in Hamburg or some other large city. Nerves were edgy ever since my incarceration in the concentration camp and the outlook for leaving Germany in the near future looked bleak. Letting things ride was also not the thing to do. I had applied for emigration to America but was waiting for a reply. Somewhere, somehow I had to find an interim country where I could wait for my American visa to be issued.

I decided to take a trip to the beautiful city of Hamburg where many nations had their representatives. It was the most frustrating trip I ever undertook. No foreign countries were interested in us. We were the outcasts of society, just as Hitler had labelled us.

Some countries generously offered us visas if we could show them visas issued by other countries already. If you had an American visa, they too would issue you a temporary visa. Who needed that? The important thing was to get the first visa which nobody was willing to issue! Very downhearted and disappointed I returned to Nordhausen still in search of a foreign visa. By now I almost did not care where I went or to which country.

My mother regularly phoned her sister in Vienna, Austria, and mentioned the problems I was having in obtaining a visa to an interim country.

A short while later we received a phone call from my uncle telling us that he would be able to get me a visa in Vienna via one of the many travel agencies doing business in the city. The only prerequisite was that I had to mail him my passport.

A German passport was a very valuable document, especially to us Jews at the time. I hated to part with it but my uncle assured me that this was common practice and I should not worry about it. In desperation I decided to post my passport by registered mail, hoping that it would be returned to me within about two weeks. This would represent the first step in my emigration to America.

Nordhausen's newspaper was of the conservative kind and a typical small-town newspaper. Their headlines were dull, unless something very special happened in this world of ours; yet by Nordhausen's standards this happened very rarely. My passport had now been gone for about ten days. My hopes were high and optimistic until a newspaper headline stared me in the face in big black letters: 'Counterfeit Passport Mill Raided in Vienna'. Thousands of foreign passports were seized. I broke out in a cold sweat. Without knowing any details I knew I was somehow involved in this scheme.

Several phone calls later to my uncle in Vienna confirmed what I feared; my passport was among the thousands seized.

Luckily enough my passport was returned to me by post about a week after the raid had taken place with a letter from the police department in Vienna.

I was happy to have my passport back in my possession but obtaining a visa to an interim country was still impossible and this was another disappointment in a long list of disappointments!

Another Gestapo raid took place last night. This time they arrested Jewish individuals or families whose emigration had made little progress. They also arrested some wealthy families.

The Gestapo's scheme was to force those Jews who still had no definite emigration plans to sign up to go to Shanghai, China. If they had no money to pay for such a trip, the wealthy families who had been arrested were forced to pay for the passages of these people. After everybody had signed on the dotted line, the Gestapo released them.

My aim was to emigrate to the United States of America. Being forced to emigrate to Shanghai would lead me in the wrong direction. My parents decided to remain in Germany.

Through underground channels we heard that there were ways and means of being smuggled into Belgium. A secret meeting was held and four people, including me, signed up for this adventure to get into Belgium via the 'black border'. We all had our passports and all our German documents were approved. What we lacked was a foreign visa. Our party was made up of Julius and Lucy Feist, Hermann Arndt and myself. I knew the Feists well as they were part of our congregation in Nordhausen, and my parents knew Hermann Arndt. We left Nordhausen by express train to the city of Cologne which was the first step closer to our goal.

In Cologne we stayed overnight with friends who were most helpful in advising us of the pros and cons of this adventure. Many of their friends had successfully gone this route and were safely in Belgium.

The main danger was getting caught in the border regions of Belgium as the Belgian authorities would send you back to the German side of the fence. We had to get to Brussels and, once there, had to contact the police who would issue documents that permitted us to stay a minimum of six months. This could be extended indefinitely.

Our Cologne friends knew of a 'reliable' smuggler who we had to contact in a certain coffee house in the city. Luckily, on the day we went there, he happened to be in the coffee house and we started negotiations with him immediately. His fee was RM500.00 per person, payable in advance. In return he would guide us to the Belgian border region and we would try to make it safely out of Germany.

We arranged a date, paid the man his fee and waited for his explicit instructions on how to proceed. We arranged a second meeting at the coffee house and worried whether he would show up or whether he had taken off with our money. When our smuggler, Louis, showed up promptly it gave us much needed confidence.

He told us to take the express train from Cologne to Aachen on 14 March 1939. There we were to transfer to a local train that would take us to Monschau, a tiny town high in the Eifel Mountains, which was the official border crossing station between Germany and Belgium in that region. One stop before Monschau was a small town called Kalterherberg, which was where Louis would contact us.

We had an uneventful trip to Aachen and transferred, as we had been told, onto the local train and at the first stop, still in the outskirts of Aachen, Gestapo agents surrounded the whole train. They arrested all of us who had intended to cross the border illegally. This was a popular place for people to cross the border illegally, and the Gestapo were always on the lookout for people trying to do this.

To our surprise, almost all of the passengers on this train were trying the same method we had chosen to leave Germany! Outside the railroad station long lines of streetcars were waiting for us. They loaded us onto them and took us back to the main station in Aachen, where they forced us to buy tickets back to Cologne. The Gestapo took away our passports but promised to return them once we had arrived in Cologne.

We were told never to use this escape route again or we would end up back in the concentration camp of Buchenwald. They meant business! Our passports were the most valuable possessions we had but, amazingly, the Gestapo kept their promise and returned our passports in Cologne.

Two days later Louis contacted us again in the coffee house. He had heard about the Gestapo raid and had come up with a completely revised plan which was as follows: we were to split into groups of two and go by train to a small town about halfway between Cologne and Aachen. Upon arrival there, we were to transfer onto a postal omnibus which would take us through the 'Siegfried Line' to Kalterherberg. We would disembark there and take the train from Kalterherberg to Monschau, where we were to meet in the station restaurant. Julius and Lucy Feist were to make the trip in the morning while Hermann Arndt and I would undertake the trip in the afternoon. In order not to lose any more time, we scheduled our departure for the next day.

As arranged we took the train and transferred to the postal omnibus. We had a wait of about an hour and to be as inconspicuous as possible, we took the seats in the very last row of the bus. Slowly the bus filled up and, just before departure, the Gestapo boarded the vehicle to check the identity of every passenger and the purpose of their trip. After all, this was highly secret defence territory, it was the area of the Siegfried Line of defence. We went through agony until the two Gestapo agents finally reached us. They checked our passports which were in order. We told them that we wanted to try going over the border into Belgium. One of the agents winked at us and wished us good luck! With that the agents left the bus and gave the driver of the bus the go-ahead to start his run. Wow, that was a close call! We could only ascribe this to pure luck, as we had been arrested the time before. Perhaps it was because we were leaving Germany legally, despite the fact that we would be entering Belgium illegally. Would 17 March 1939 be a luckier day than the 14th?

As we started our bus trip it began to rain very hard, and as the bus went higher the rain became sleet and snow. It was not just an ordinary snowstorm; it turned into a blizzard. Our bus was struggling to go around the hairpin bends, its rear-wheels spinning and sliding back and forth. Would we be able to stop if necessary or would we skid into any obstacle in our way? The trip became a nightmare!

Eventually we reached Kalterherberg, and had to wade to the railroad station through deep snow to catch the train to Monschau. We struggled to climb the road to the station. We were not dressed properly for the weather but eventually made it in time and boarded the train. When we arrived at Monschau total chaos prevailed. Due to the blizzard all the electricity was out and official offices had to operate by candlelight. The German customs officials processed us quickly as all our papers were in order. We asked the agents to show us the way to the station restaurant to make sure that we did not mistakenly wander into the Belgian customs office as we had no paperwork allowing us to enter Belgium. Because of the electricity failure, the corridor to the restaurant was completely dark. Suddenly flashlights blinded us and two girls guided us to a side door which turned out to be the rear entrance to the kitchen of the station restaurant. The two girls were the daughters of the owner of the station restaurant and they too were in on the plan. The Feists had arrived earlier and had told them what we looked like.

Julius and Lucy Feist were sitting near the stove warming themselves. They were worried about us and were so glad to see us alive and well. Their trip was much less exciting and they got through without a hitch.

We were told to stay in the back of the kitchen until everything had quietened down. Our instructions were to follow the no-man's road outside the station to a house which belonged to Louis. The right side of this road belonged to Germany, while the left side was Belgian territory. The house would be easily recognisable as its main entrance was flanked by two large pine trees and a light would be burning high under the eaves of the roof.

This was all very well without the snow but under blizzard conditions everything looked different and there was no electricity! Where was Louis' house? The snow got deeper and deeper and we fought our way along until we came to a house that fitted Louis' description. As we were deciding a door opened and a man came out waving us in. We had, indeed, found our way into Belgian territory. Hurrah, hurrah! However, to our disappointment, we had to stay in his house until the blizzard ended as we could have perished outside in the storm!

Louis had comfortable rooms tucked under the roof. We had to keep quiet, especially if someone rang the doorbell. At night we could go out into the backyard for a breath of fresh air; the rest of the day we had to remain silent. Louis fed us very well.

Meanwhile, the snow piled higher and higher and after three days the sky cleared at last and Louis debated taking a chance in doing a five-hour hike through difficult terrain to a certain point in the woods where a taxi would be cruising up and down the highway awaiting our arrival. None of us were dressed correctly and it was Louis who had to make the decision whether or not to go. Louis decided to set out that night with the assistance of a friend.

From the beginning it became obvious that this trip would not take five hours, but closer to seven or eight hours. The snow was too deep and powdery and the going was awfully slow. We had to jump across brooks, guide ourselves by railroad tracks, and hold signal wires down with our hands so that our progress was not heard in the signal control house. We avoided areas where dogs could be alerted, walked uphill and down-hill making wide detours around military control posts and avoiding the defence fortifications of the Little Maginot Line, Belgium's first line of defence.

Louis and his assistant knew what to do and where to go, but we made painfully slow progress. As the hours dragged on our pace got slower and slower, especially that of Julius and Lucy Feist. Lucy finally became delirious and was unable to go on. Julius started slapping his wife's face, but to no avail. We were in serious trouble and we all knew it. Louis decided to split us into two groups and he remained with the Feists while his assistant took charge of Hermann Arndt and me. We cut through the woods with much greater efficiency and eventually reached the stretch of highway where our taxi was supposed to meet us. The taxi was due to pass by every twenty minutes and while we waited in the woods, our guide stood lookout near the edge of the road.

To our great amazement the taxi arrived very quickly and our guide asked the taxi-driver to do one more run to check that he was not being followed. Standing in the woods we were chilled to the bone but felt better once we entered the warm and comfortable taxi. Thus our trip to Brussels began in earnest, and we arrived in Brussels in the early hours of the morning and were taken to a Jewish deli in the centre of the city.

This deli was apparently the end of the line for refugees like us. In the backroom there were large mattresses and we dumped ourselves on one of them and fell into a deep sleep brought on from sheer exhaustion. Several hours later we woke up covered in bedbug bites and fled the place in horror.

We had to settle down in this city and had to do it quickly. My first phone call was to my cousin Charlotte Becker and her husband, Arthur, in Holland. They were delighted to hear that I was safely out of Germany and said they were willing to send me a small amount of money every month until my departure for America. My second phone call was to our contact man in Brussels informing him of our safe arrival. We also told him that Julius and Lucy Feist were in trouble in the middle of the woods and that their fate lay in the hands of Louis, our smuggler. We said we would stay in touch with him to be kept abreast of further developments. On speaking to him the following day he told us that Julius and Lucy had also arrived safely in Brussels and had been hospitalised. We found them in a wonderful Catholic hospital where the love and care of the sisters was conducive to total recovery.

Louis's helper had returned to them after he had sent us on our way to Brussels. He saw that they had no chance of getting two elderly people safely through the woods. They took Julius and Lucy to a nearby farmhouse and explained the circumstances to the farmer who called an ambulance which arrived shortly thereafter. Both were taken by ambulance to Brussels with sirens blaring and red lights flashing and dropped off at the Catholic hospital.

With not a penny to their name, Julius spent four weeks and Lucy three months at this facility recovering from hypothermia, exhaustion and frostbite.

Six months after arriving in Belgium I was fortunate enough to receive my immigration visa to the United States of America. Two or three months later Julius and Lucy Feist arrived safely in the United States to join their son. I, unfortunately, lost all contact with Hermann Arndt.

I said goodbye to my friends in Brussels on a Saturday morning. Hopefully, the next time we saw each other would be in America – the sooner the better.

I took the express train from Brussels to Amsterdam. I intended visiting Aunt Grete, my father's sister, who had emigrated to Holland earlier that year. Her husband, Uncle Seppi, unfortunately, had passed away shortly after their arrival in Holland.

When the American Consulate informed me that they would issue me with my immigration visa, I immediately got in touch with the Holland America Line and tried to book passage to New York. Since I had paid in advance, it was not complicated at all and they notified me that I would have to share a cabin with another passenger. My reservation was on the 'New Amsterdam', the flagship of the Holland America Line, all 36 000 tons of it.

The ship was to set sail on Monday evening which would give me ample time to visit Aunt Grete. The express train from Brussels to Amsterdam stopped at the border between the two countries where the customs agents inspected our papers. The Belgian agents found everything in order while the Dutch agents were not happy with my German passport. I explained to them that I was leaving for America on Monday evening, travelling on the 'New Amsterdam', a Dutch ship and that I wanted to visit my Aunt Grete in Amsterdam. They eventually took me and my luggage off the train and put me in a nondescript room in a building that was probably the Customs House. I pleaded with them, explaining over and over again that I had no intention of staying in Holland. Since the outbreak of the war things had changed and people with German passports were considered suspicious.

Several hours later they allowed me to board the next express train to Amsterdam. What changed their minds I do not know, maybe they checked with the Holland America Line and verified my statements. I had lost several valuable hours of my visit with Aunt Grete but was grateful that I was able to see her at all.

She insisted on taking me to Rotterdam on Monday in the late afternoon in order to see me off on the 'New Amsterdam'. She stuffed some money into my pocket, so I would not be without funds; the Germans permitted you to travel with only RM10.00, which in today's terms is worth US$3!

When we arrived at the dock we were notified that the ship was not sailing on Monday as scheduled as the crew was on strike and wanted 'hazard pay', due to the many ships being torpedoed by German U-boats. Aunt Grete went back to Amsterdam and I found myself a cheap room near the harbour in the hope that we would leave the next day. It took a whole week before the strike was settled. My funds were depleted and I arrived in New York City with US$3 after all!

My cabin mate turned out to be an American newspaper reporter who, unfortunately, spoke too quickly with a strange accent. I could not follow his English but somehow we still made ourselves understood.

Thank G'd, the trip across the Atlantic was uneventful except for one day when Mother Nature let go with full fury and our ship moaned and groaned. My fellow passenger still got dressed in a snow-white tailored suit and went upstairs to have some breakfast. Less than ten minutes later he returned with coffee spilled all over his beautiful suit. He returned to bed, called our steward and asked what he would prescribe to counteract seasickness. Our steward, an experienced sailor of many years, ordered us a huge bowl of fresh fruit and a plate of sandwiches and cold milk to drink. Believe it or not, we did not get seasick.

The waves that struck the ship were so high they had to place ropes all over the ship for the passengers to hold onto. No food was served in the dining rooms. The American's beautiful white suit went to the dry-cleaners, but I never saw him wearing it again. The next day the ocean was as smooth as glass and after one week of travelling we sailed into New York harbour and past the Statue of Liberty. What a euphoric sight to welcome us as we began a new life as newly arrived immigrants.

The 'New Amsterdam' did not return to Europe but stayed in America and was used for cruises to the Caribbean. Later, when America entered World War II and required ships for troop transports, the 'New Amsterdam' was gutted and used for this purpose. Being modern and fast, this ship could travel without a destroyer escort.

After the end of the war, the ship was refitted to its original beauty and sailed the seven seas for many more years. The Dutch built a new 'New Amsterdam', twice the size of the old one, and the old flagship was retired and decommissioned. I feel nostalgic about the old 'New Amsterdam'; after all it was instrumental in bringing me to the shores of America, where a totally new life started for the Herrmann family.

Life in America

Upon arrival in America I settled down, found a job in a glove factory and lived with Johnny and Margot Stern who were close friends of my parents. Johnny was our former doctor in Nordhausen. We lived very harmoniously together. Johnny allowed me to drive his brand new automobile which enabled me to welcome many former friends and acquaintances at the harbour upon their arrival in America.

War broke out with Germany on 7 December 1941 and in 1942 I received an invitation from 'Uncle Sam' to become a soldier in the US armed forces.

I received basic training in Kentucky and upon conclusion of this, I was granted US citizenship. I was transferred to Camp Ritchie, Maryland, to be prepared for special training. Because I could speak German, I was trained in various types of intelligence work – interrogation of prisoners of war, administering a captured city, identifying aerial photography and many other facets of this type of work. Upon completion of our training we were all sent off to Europe without definite assignment.

Passover 1944

The army shipped us to Northern Ireland to wait for our eventual assignment to a definite unit. We were stationed in a small town about an hour away from Belfast, the largest town in Northern Ireland. Ignoramus that I was, I never associated Northern Ireland with any kind of Jewish population. But I was proven wrong! When it came close to Passover, a buddy of mine asked me if I would be interested in attending a Seder at his distant relative's home in Belfast. He had permission from his relatives to bring five friends to the Seder. I accepted promptly, provided I would be issued a pass, which turned out to be a cinch.

We travelled in a festive mood to Belfast to meet our host who was a very orthodox Jew and when he welcomed us as his guests he had only one request, that we accompany him to synagogue, a request we could hardly deny. Belfast had been under heavy air attacks from the German air force and damage was visible everywhere. Lately the attacks had ceased; apparently the American air strength had made itself felt.

When we went to the synagogue we passed through an area of great devastation but, lo and behold, the synagogue stood intact among the ruins, completely undamaged! I think there is a G'd who spreads out his arms to protect those He loves. After the service our host introduced us to many of his friends in the congregation. I think he was showing off a bit with all us American boys who were guests at his family's Seder, but he did a mitzvah for us who otherwise would not have celebrated Pesach at all.

The Seder was conducted in a very Orthodox manner. Not a word was left out and it took some time until we reached the page in the Hagadah, where it says 'And now you may eat the Seder dinner'. Our host knew all the melodies and his explanations of the exodus of the Jews from Egypt were lengthy and thorough but we finally reached the Passover meal.

Let me assure you it was worth waiting for! The food was delicious in every respect and these people made us feel at home – a rare talent indeed. It was a large Seder gathering: Our host, his wife, their sons and daughters and their husbands and wives and all the grandchildren and, last but not least, we six GIs.

During the dinner we had lively conversations with our hosts and we GIs had to tell them all about our lives in America. They wanted to know what the future held in store for us and what our aspirations were. We talked about politics and, of course, about the war.

Finishing our sumptuous meal, we resumed our duties to complete the Seder. We were in a good mood and sang along to the old traditional melodies. It was a great evening and wonderful experience!

Since our hosts had a very large house, they were able to accommodate us for the night and the next morning we went to synagogue, as promised.

During the afternoon the son-in-law drove us through Belfast to show us part of the city. Since gasoline was strictly rationed and available by coupon only, they must have purchased some on the black-market to enable them to do this.

That night there was a second Seder, just as fantastic as the first one and we went to synagogue again next morning. Eventually the holiday was over and we went back to camp.

After our stay in Northern Ireland, we were shipped all over Great Britain, where our main purpose was to instruct our own troops in what to expect once they were engaged with the enemy. Luckily enough, I was not involved in the invasion of Europe but later on our unit was transferred to France to continue our intelligence work.

I had a lucky break when I got assigned to the Third US Army headquarters of General Patton. There we were engaged in the interrogation of prisoners of war and our daily report became a must-read item for all those who had clearance to read top-secret material.

The Ner Tamid in Arlon, Belgium

We were on the move, as one usually is, if one has an illustrious General in command. Our orders were to take up quarters in the city of Arlon in Belgium. Arlon was a small town of perhaps 10 000 to 12 000 inhabitants. Its only importance in the war was that it was a strategic railroad hub and that several highways intersected there.

It was customary for us, whenever time permitted, to walk through a town looking at anything worthwhile, be it an ancient church, an old city hall or a half-timbered building but this little town really was not very interesting.

The population was very insecure and scared. They had been under Nazi occupation for a long time before we liberated the city, only to have it fall under Nazi occupation once more during the Battle of the Ardennes, also known as the Battle of the Bulge. Now we had liberated this town again, this time hopefully for good.

My buddy, Kurt Loebel, and I walked down a long street of houses and suddenly noticed a building that looked like it could be a synagogue. How could this be? The Nazis had been so efficient in destroying synagogues throughout Europe. We went to the house next door and found that we were correct. We asked the man where we could find a key to the synagogue. He directed us to the door of a frightened old lady and we asked her to let us have a look at the synagogue. She came with us to the synagogue and told us that they no longer held services as only three Jewish men and six Jewish women had returned to Arlon and they lacked a proper *minyan*.

When we arrived at the synagogue the lady unlocked the door and as we entered this house of worship we were simply speechless. This little synagogue was completely intact. We were amazed that anything remained after Hitler's storm troopers had been in the city.

This little synagogue was simply a gem. The *bima* was located at the centre, with benches for worshippers all around it, and a beautiful *Aron ha-Kodesh*. This house of worship just sent out a glow of warmth the moment you entered it.

We told the lady to alert all Jewish people in town to be at the synagogue the following Friday night. We would hold Shabbat services and would take care of the *minyan*. We notified our army chaplain who in turn sent out notices to all units stationed in or near Arlon giving the Jewish soldiers the opportunity to attend Friday night services at the synagogue of Arlon. Transportation would be furnished by the unit commanders.

Friday night came and the little synagogue rapidly filled to capacity. The doors were kept open so those unable to find seats could also participate.

Our chaplain conducted a beautiful Friday night service after the *Ner Tamid* was relit. The old traditional melodies echoed through the building and services were concluded with an *Oneg Shabbat*. Thereafter we presented some meagre presents to the nine Jewish inhabitants of Arlon. We sacrificed some of our PX-rations, such as chocolate bars, cigarettes, pipe-tobacco, toothpaste, etc., and our mess-sergeant contributed some food he could spare. The nine Jewish inhabitants of Arlon went home loaded with goodies.

We were stationed in Arlon for about four weeks and every Friday night services were held in the little synagogue. When we left Arlon we notified the troops following us and it can be safely assumed that they too held their Friday night services in the little synagogue of Arlon.

Those Jewish soldiers who attended the rites of relighting the *Ner Tamid* in Arlon, Belgium will never forget the emotional impact that this service had on us. Many a GI had a lump in their throat or a misty eye.

A return to Nordhausen, 17th April 1945

In 1945, while stationed in Freising, a city near Munich, I was able to visit my home town of Nordhausen. I was hoping to be able to collect some information on the fate of my dear parents. The outlook was grim. Through the interrogation of prisoners of war, we heard terrible stories about what was done to the Jewish people throughout Europe. Was there a chance that my parents survived at all? And would this trip to Nordhausen yield any clues?

I approached Nordhausen from the direction of Sondershausen, which was badly damaged from bombing runs by the air forces. It was a bit hazy, as it sometimes is in the Helmetal and Nordhausen looked a bit strange from a distance but I could not understand why. As I got closer to the city I saw that the airport was completely wrecked and all the newly erected barracks had been bombed to hell. Nordhausen was home to the largest factory in Germany that produced the V-1 and V-2 rockets. It has to be assumed that this fact contributed to making Nordhausen an important target for the Allied Forces and led to the destruction of the city. Nordhausen was completely devastated on 3 and 4 April 1945 – about two weeks before our forces occupied and liberated the city.

After the railway underpass, I turned left into the Lange Strasse where everything seemed to be in fairly good shape, as was the railway station with its ugly architectural design. All the hotels at the Bahnhofsplatz were intact.

I decided to drive north on the Bahnhofstrasse and arrived at the bridge over the Zorge River where the scene suddenly changed completely. From that point on, the city of Nordhausen simply no longer existed.

The streets were filled with debris and rubbish from the ruins of the big houses that used to line the Bahnhofstrasse. All the streets had been destroyed and all that remained of a town with a history of more than a thousand years was a huge pile of rubble.

19b Bahnhofstrasse, amazingly, was not completely wrecked. This was the last house I had lived in before emigrating and where I said my final goodbyes to my beloved parents and dear grandmother. The building was now uninhabitable, windows and doors were missing as a result of the bomb blasts; parts of the walls were badly damaged and there was no roof.

I turned left into the Arnoldstrasse to go deeper into the city and passed the house where my parents were forced live before their deportation. It was one of the 'Jew houses', as they were known. They had been forced to move there by the Nazis. I had received mail from this address before my parents were deported. All that was left were four empty walls, the rest of the house was burnt out.

I went up to the Gehegeplatz where the city council was located. I wanted to find out whether Hermann Twelkemeier, my cousin Edith's father, had survived. I thought he might know something about the fate of my dear parents. I enquired with the authorities whether any lists existed with names of inhabitants of the city but the answer was no; everything had been burned to ashes.

A crowd formed around me when people realised I was an American soldier who could speak German. Someone pointed out a man, Paul Strieber, who seemed to know everybody, the relationships of the various families, etc. I asked him to join me and he sat with my driver and me in our vehicle and told us what had happened in Nordhausen. He was extremely well informed, knew every family, where they used to live, how they were related to each other, where they emigrated to, etc. Not only did I ask him a lot of questions, but he was just as interested to hear how Dr Sterns was doing in America, or what became of the Walter Eisners, what happened to Max Heilbruns and so forth.

He was able to provide me with the address of Hermann Twelkemeier, who lived at Reichsstrasse on the corner of Landgrabenstrassse, one of the few buildings undamaged in the bombing raids.

I asked Mr Strieber if the Jewish cemetery still existed since I wanted to visit the graves of my grandparents. He replied that the cemetery was still there, but you could only get to it if you were willing to climb over the debris in and around all the bomb craters.

By now it was lunchtime and we drove over the 'Ring' to the Rosarium, a public rose garden, opened the gate, drove in and sat down to eat our lunch. In the far distance we could hear the thunder of the guns up in the Harz Mountains where the fighting was still in progress. The Harz Mountains looked beautiful from the 'Schöne Aussicht' and the 'Kirschallee'. Incongruously, everything was in bloom throughout the destroyed city.

We found it very hard to get to the area near the cemetery and finally parked our Jeep and took off on foot, climbing over piles of rocks, around huge craters until we eventually reached the gate. The right side of the cemetery was intact but the left side had been almost destroyed by a direct hit from a 500-pound bomb. The War Memorial had prevented certain graves from being destroyed, and diminished the force of the blast to a certain extent. The cemetery gardener's house and the Memorial Hall were still there but badly battered.

As I walked down the path, an old woman, followed by an even older man, came towards me. It was Mr and Mrs Petri, who took care of the graves. When I told them which graves I wanted to visit, they recognised me and broke down, tears running down their cheeks, crying like children, embracing me and kissing me. It was very moving. They too told me a little more about what had happened and how good the cemetery had looked and how they had taken care of it until the day when everything went to pieces. I gave them some money to fix up the cemetery as best they could and told them to go to the Military Government and ask for some assistance when things had quietened down a bit. Many emigrants have their dear ones buried in the cemetery in Nordhausen. I was not able to find the graves of Theodor and Else Herrmann, my father's oldest brother and his wife. However, my grandparents' graves were in very good condition.

I saw a lot of destruction in Germany, in big cities and smaller ones, but I think that in no other place was the destruction as complete as in my home town.

We drove downtown again to contact Hermann Twelkemeier. This time we chose the Hohnsteinerstrasse, one of the few streets which was still fairly intact. Here and there a house was gone but the area looked more like it used to. When we reached the house where it said in big letters 'H. Twelkemeier', I entered the apartment and a family who were living in the house, asked me 'Vous parlez Francais?' Well, I made sure that I was in the correct apartment. Indeed I was. These French-speaking people were just put into the apartment while Hermann was away. I think they must have been slave labourers from a concentration camp called Dora, which was near Nordhausen. I then went upstairs and an old lady opened the door, her face looked familiar to me. She also did not know Hermann's whereabouts and so I decided to write a short letter and leave it with the French people. While I composed the letter, the old lady told me that she had been in America and had a brother living in Providence, Rhode Island. This sounded familiar to me and she told me that she too was bombed out and lost practically everything. Full of interest, I asked her where she used to live and realised that she was Mrs Witt, our landlady from our previous apartment on the Bahnhoffstrasse. She turned pale and I was afraid she would faint on me. 'I know you', she said, 'your face seems so familiar.' And then it clicked! 'You are Kurt Herrmann!' She broke down in tears and there were no words to calm her down. She told me of the last days of my parents in Nordhausen. She had given my mother some extra stockings to take along for the journey. My mother was going to write to her, to let her know where they were shipped. But the letter never came. My parents were marched off to the freight railway station in the middle of the night, told how much baggage to bring, what size it had to be, and how it had to be marked. They were put onto coaches and all their baggage was put into a luggage car. It never joined them, and their meagre possessions were stolen. From there they were sent to Theresienstadt.

We met up with Mr Strieber once again and he estimated that between 6 000 and 8 000 people in Nordhausen were killed in the air attacks and that there were no more than 22 000 inhabitants left from a former population of 43 000.

It was time to leave; we still had a very long trip back and we turned into the Erfurterstrasse to reach the highway that would take us back to my unit. Going up the Windleite I took a last look at the big rubbish pile that once used to be the city of Nordhausen that had ceased to exist.

My trip to the ghetto of Theresienstadt

After the end of the war, I decided to visit the ghetto of Theresienstadt to try to find out the fate of my parents. It became known that many German Jews were sent there, and it seemed the best place to start to try and discover what had happened to my family. Theresienstadt had originally been a Czech garrison town and had a population of about 8 000 people. The Germans took it over and turned it into a ghetto to house Jews before they were sent to the camps. It housed about 60 000 people during this time.

A fellow soldier and I, who both did not know the fate of our parents, finally got permission to try to cross the demarcation line between the Russian and American armies in order to reach the ghetto of Theresienstadt, 45 km north of Prague.

We had some letters of recommendation written in Russian for our allies which we thought would help us get across the demarcation line. We even had a Jeep and driver officially assigned to us. With the letters in our pockets and the good wishes of our friends, we took off one Saturday afternoon. The weather was rather unfriendly, much the same as the purpose of our trip and it did nothing to improve our spirits.

We sped along but having left comparatively late, we only reached the Czech border late and decided to spend the night in the little town of Eisenstein.

We were so glad to have left German territory. The atmosphere in Germany was not good and being in a country where one could act freely was delightful.

We met the mayor of the town who arranged accommodation for us in a teacher's house. We walked around the little town and found a pleasant restaurant where there was a dance going on in honour of the Czech army which had only arrived recently. We invited ourselves and were greeted as very welcome guests. I danced a few rounds but found that my legs were stiff from not having danced since leaving England. Quite tired, we returned to our accommodation where our hostess had baked a cake and brewed us some pretty good *ersatzkaffee*.

The next morning we set off via Pilsen to Prague. We got to our outpost, and were stopped by a PFC on duty who wanted to see our passes. We told him of our intentions but he would not let us pass. His sergeant of the guard was sitting there, sunbathing, and we showed him the three letters written in Russian and our letters of recommendation. Our story impressed him so much, that he gave us the go-ahead. There was a short stretch of no-man's land before we reached the Russian outpost. We stopped and showed the guard the letter meant for him. We offered him a cigarette and with that gesture, friendship was established. This was the procedure at the rest of the outposts we passed through on our way to Prague. It all went remarkably smoothly.

We finally reached Prague and after another hour's drive arrived at the gates of Theresienstadt. The first place we came to was a concentration camp much like the others where they imprisoned all kinds of people for various reasons.

A little further along we came to the main gates of the ghetto of Theresienstadt. Big signs had been put up, stating 'Typhus' but this did not stop us from entering. We were shown to the Registrar where two female staffers assisted us as we went to work on the files. These were neatly kept sets of file-cards on which the information of every single inmate still in Theresienstadt was recorded. During the war they had the finest filing system imaginable with the names of everybody who had been incarcerated there. However, these records had been burnt just before the Russians arrived to liberate Theresienstadt and the only cards left now were those of the inmates still incarcerated there.

I had made a long list of names of people I wanted to look up but very soon I realised that they were no longer in this place. I was not able to find a single name of those that I tried to locate.

However, I was introduced to a number of people working in the offices and gleaned the following information:

My parents were deported to Auschwitz, Poland, in October 1944, where I must assume they were gassed. I tried to find out the date of death of my grandmother, Lea Moses, my mother's mother, but this turned out to be impossible.

In autumn of the previous year, 1944, 20 000 people were shipped in several trainloads to Auschwitz where they were sorted like cattle into good and bad specimens. Of the above number, 5 000 people were found fit enough to be placed into work camps, the other 15 000 were gassed to death. We can only assume that no elderly people escaped the gas chamber.

As it was explained to us, the process of gassing was a mechanical affair. The poor victim's entire body was shaved; they then entered the so-called 'shower', where they stood under a gadget which looked like a showerhead. Upon order the tap was opened and instead of water, gas poured out and killed the person instantly. A wide open mouth was a sign that the victim had died. The corpse was moved one floor down where it fell automatically into the fire. Children usually were thrown into the fire alive without being gassed we were told. Certain ingredients of the body were then used to make soap. One can assume that the hair was also used.

The few people left in Theresienstadt were mostly men and women of mixed marriages who had only arrived there recently. We were able to get a fairly complete list of all German Jews who remained in Theresienstadt which amounted to exactly 5 193 persons. That night we made copies of the list which would be forwarded to the different Jewish agencies in America.

Let me tell you a bit about the ghetto Theresienstadt in general. It was a small town which had a normal peacetime population of about 7 000 inhabitants. It was an old garrison town and fortifications with huge walls and ditches surrounded the whole place. You could walk from one end of town to the other in five to ten minutes. It was an 'ideal' place to incarcerate people. It effectively served as a holding place for Jews before they were sent to various extermination camps, and many people who were held there perished in Auschwitz.

The Jews tried to beautify the town. There were two parks, a coffee house, a bank, a post-office and a bakery. All other buildings were living quarters. There are some big permanent stone barracks located in the city; after all it was a garrison-town. The rest of Theresienstadt consisted of ordinary houses. This small city housed as many as 60 000 inmates at one time and they all had to find a space to stay. From the outside the streets and houses looked like any Czech city or town but when you looked behind the walls and saw what was going on inside, it left you speechless. People were forced to live under the most primitive conditions, with little sanitation for example. Add the awful smell and serious outbreaks of illnesses and you will get the picture. There was no family life whatsoever because men and women were housed separately. Women were not permitted to bear children and if a woman fell pregnant, mother and child were shipped to Auschwitz and gassed.

I went into the quarters of some of the barracks and looked through the windows of some of the homes and the sight left me with a sick feeling in my stomach. There was a stench hanging over the whole city that made you feel nauseous.

Inmates were fed in community kitchens and every block had its own set-up. Food was very scarce and the Jews were put on a starvation diet under Nazi orders, with the result that many of the elderly people simply starved to death. Of course, once the Russians liberated the ghetto they all had plenty to eat and sometimes even had a surplus of rations on hand.

One of the terrible streets was the Bahnhofstrasse where the trains stopped in the street, either to discharge the new arrivals or to take away the poor victims to their unknown destination. I happened to see a train that had just returned from Hungary and had brought back the first transport of Jews to their home towns. The train was being cleaned and the whole street was full of trash and garbage and the stench was unbearable.

We walked through the whole town and spoke to people who explained all the different functions of each house and barracks and cave, etc. and one could only describe it as a truly horrible sight.

The inmates lived under such terrible conditions, but to them it became their reality. They would tell you 'my mother was gassed in Auschwitz' or 'my husband was killed in Buchenwald' like any normal person would say 'I saw a nice movie last night'. One person explained to me that they had to climb the stairs very slowly or they would lose too much weight due to the poor and insufficient meals they received during the war.

I saw skeletons walking about supporting themselves on big sticks – they were victims of a concentration camp and had just arrived in Theresienstadt, pale as a white sheet of paper, their eyes without any expression, talking to themselves.

There were children, little boys and girls, and the elderly, all moving about aimlessly.

That was one part of the population. The other part consisted of well-dressed men in fine-tailored suits and nicely patterned ties and the women wore lipstick and acted as if they were in a summer resort. These were mostly Czech Jews. The tragedy of this place was that the Nazis were able to create real hatred between the various Jewish factions; the Dutch Jews could not stand the French Jews, the German Jews could not stand the Czech Jews, the Belgian Jews could not stand the Polish Jews, etc. They did this by forcing one group of Jews, for example the Dutch Jews, to put forward the names of people to be sent to the camps when the Gestapo decided it was time to send another 'transport'. Of course each group would want to save themselves and therefore they complied. In this way the Gestapo succeeded in splitting up the various groups, so they could not band together. Sadly, all of them were facing the same fate; they had been sentenced to death according to the Nazi decree and it was only a matter of who would be killed first.

When people realised that we were Americans, we were surrounded by several hundred inmates. It was such a pitiful sight and it is so hard to describe the real spirit of this place; one actually had to see it to believe it. They threw their letters into our Jeep in the hope that we could mail them; but how could we explain to these desperate people that we could only send mail through army postal channels.

During the war before the great evacuation to Auschwitz took place, Red Cross officials were sent to inspect the camp. The whole city had to look nice and neat from the outside. The SS sent several hundred evening dresses and tuxedoes to the camp and a big ball was arranged with dancing, an orchestra, a variety show and all the trimmings! Two days later the first transports left for Auschwitz. The inmates were told they were being put to work and everyone was willing to go. For them it turned out to be a trip into Hell.

We spent the whole afternoon and the next morning in the ghetto of Theresienstadt and it was a relief for all of us when we could leave it again knowing we had fulfilled our mission.

The next day we met Dr Leo Baeck, the former chief rabbi of Berlin. He was very happy to see us and he was so emotionally touched that tears came to his eyes. The man was 72 years of age and it was a wonder that he lived through it all. He looked very sick and old and was no longer the same man who once spoke up for the Jews of Germany. He still went about his business but to us he seemed a broken man.

He was working with Dr Merziger, another leading personality and together they were assisting the Jews of Theresienstadt.

The main problem arose due to the fact that the ghetto of Theresienstadt had to be liquidated as soon as possible. All the people had to go back to their home towns. During our stay the last Dutch Jews were repatriated by air.

The problem now was the German Jews. The few who remained did not want to go back to Germany with the exception of those who had Gentile spouses or children waiting for them. We were told there were about 2 000 Jews who had nobody in Germany they could go back to. They did not want to be shipped back to a country that had caused them so much misery. For those 2 000 Jews ways and means had to be found to get them into America or Canada. One could do a great deed if this information was forwarded to the right places and channels.

The Czech and Russian authorities who ran the ghetto of Theresien-stadt at the end of the war did everything possible to help those people and they did a fine and remarkable job.

I had taken along some candy bars, army rations, cigarettes, soap and chewing gum, and when I gave the people the box, they behaved like children receiving a new toy.

We had completed the trip of a lifetime in our army career. This trip was successful in certain respects because it cleared the uncertainty of the fate of my parents. It was very sad but I joined the ranks of tens of thousands of others who experienced the same fate of having lost their dear ones this tragic way. We say Kaddisch for them now and keep them in our memory as we knew them at the time we had to leave them behind.

The Poplar Allee

My Uncle Willi and Aunt Marthl Griessmeier were the last outside contacts my parents had after their deportation to the ghetto Theresienstadt. They lived in Munich and everyone wondered if they would deport Aunt Marthl who was Jewish. Christian Uncle Willi had enough guts and influence to prevent her deportation. She was forced by the Nazis to clean streetcars and public toilets in Munich, but somehow she survived the Holocaust.

The end of the war in 1945 had brought nothing but disappointment for our family; it seemed nobody had survived the Holocaust. The search for one more part of the family was my duty but my hopes of finding them alive were not great after my disappointment at Theresienstadt when I did not find any of my family members alive.

I was near Munich when the war ended and I started searching for the Griessmeiers immediately. I drove my Jeep into town and looked for their house. I found the house all right, but where it once stood, there was only a huge crater.

Was I preparing to face another disaster? I went to the nearby police station and enquired about the fate of this family. The Germans, being so precise, found them at once in their files and told me that they were evacuated to a small inn at Oberaudorf, a little resort village on the German/Austrian border at the foot of the Alps.

Bombed-out Munich looked terrible; no water, no gas, no electricity. Of course, there were no public telephones either. For me there was only one thing to do if I wanted to find Uncle Willi and Aunt Marthl, I had to leave for Oberaudorf at once.

126

Thanks to the Bavarian Reichsautobahn network I got to the border rather quickly. I found the inn and inquired about the Griessmeiers at the desk. I was told they were doing well and still lived at the inn. They were not at home as they had gone to the city swimming pool. They were expected back very soon, as a big thunderstorm was approaching. I enquired where the swimming pool was located and was told it was not very far and they would use the pedestrian Poplar Allee to come home.

Poplars, being tall trees, cannot be missed even from a distance and before long I was driving down the Poplar Allee in my excitement, even though it was meant for pedestrians only. Far down the road in the distance, I spotted an elderly couple walking briskly towards me. They were obviously in a hurry and did not want to get wet in the thunderstorm.

The lightning and thunder put on a beautiful display and in the mountains it echoed rather frighteningly. I drove a bit faster down the empty Poplar Allee towards them and finally reached a point where I could make out their faces. Sure enough, it was Willi and Martha Griessmeier, who had survived the war, the Holocaust and the bombings!

I brought my Jeep to a halt right next to them and they looked at me with rather serious faces and I stared back at them. 'Climb into my Jeep, Aunt Marthl and Uncle Willi,' I said. 'You do not seem to recognise me in this American Army uniform. I am Kurt Herrmann.' They let out a yell, as only Bavarians can do. They hugged me and kissed me and embraced me, tears streaming down their faces.

Finally, they climbed into my Jeep and we raced back towards the inn and got there just in time to avoid a very heavy thunderstorm that would have soaked us to the bone.

After settling down from all the excitement they told to me that they were very upset when they saw an American army Jeep driving towards them on their Poplar Allee. 'What chutzpah these 'Amis' have, driving their vehicles on a road strictly meant for pedestrians only!'

The thunderstorm lasted a long time and gave us the opportunity to talk about many things including what had happened to their two sons, Kurt and Heinz. A problem arose for their family because Aunt Marthl was Jewish and Uncle Willi was Christian. That fact made their children either half Jewish or half Christian according to Nazi doctrine. This was to cause great tragedy for this family.

The older son, Kurt, wanted to become a lawyer but with the enforcement of the Nuremberg Laws, the universities threw obstacle after obstacle in his path. Under Nazi rule he was not able to enrol at any university. Kurt started to hate his mother, not because she was a disciplinarian but because she was a Jewess. His hatred never ceased until the day he died some years later, despite the fact that he was able to complete his studies after the war and became a lawyer.

The younger son, Heinz, was a wonderful son who loved and adored his mother. He could not do enough to please her. This somehow made up for the hatred his brother Kurt displayed. Heinz was drafted into the German army and eventually ended up on the Eastern Front somewhere in Russia. Unfortunately, he was wounded in battle and was sent back to Germany to recuperate.

The authorities notified his parents that their wounded son would arrive in Munich on an army Red Cross hospital train. Aunt Marthl did not know how badly hurt he was and, with great apprehension, went to the railroad station.

The train eventually rolled to a stop and discharged its cargo of wounded German soldiers. Marthl looked high and low for her Heinz but he was nowhere to be seen. Eventually, she started looking and searching for him in every compartment until she found a corpse in one compartment. Heinz's dead body was propped up with a large sign around his neck which said: 'Heartiest greetings to your Jewish mother'. His own comrades had murdered him. He too was another victim of the Holocaust.

Aunt Marthl and Uncle Willi moved back to Munich four weeks after I found them in Oberaudorf where they were given the apartment of a former Nazi big shot. I visited them as often as time permitted bringing them goodies from either the PX or the army kitchen. Uncle Willi would hike into the woods to bring back some kindling wood in order to make a little fire in the kitchen-stove and Aunt Marthl would prepare a meal with lots of ingenuity. Munich was still a city without gas or electricity and was a bombed-out shell.

This was a very successful mission and it was, with great satisfaction, that I was able to notify our relatives everywhere that Marthl and Willi Griessmeier had survived and were in good health. They were the only survivors of our immediate family.

The driving instructor and his wife

In 1948 I made the big switch and moved from New York to Los Angeles and never regretted it. I drove by car and made it a leisurely excursion to the West Coast. In Chicago I stopped off to visit some good old friends; I also could not resist visiting the Grand Canyon. It was an interesting trip, after all I crossed a whole continent, but it was also strenuous, sitting in the car and trying to cover 500 miles per day. At that time there were no freeways or parkways or turnpikes, it was all highway driving, at times very monotonous. It made you realise what a vast country America is. As varied as the scenery was, so were its inhabitants.

Eventually I arrived in Los Angeles, and I was welcomed by Claude and his parents. Right in the beginning an incident would determine my future life.

Claude's mother was taking driving lessons and she asked me if I was willing to practise with her a bit so she would not constantly stall the motor whenever she found herself stopped at the slightest incline. I agreed.

She was enrolled in a driving school and her progress was rather slow. Not being a driving instructor, I explained things to her in my own way, which seemed to make sense.

After our training session, which she thought was very fruitful, she put it to me this way: 'Kurt, you are a born driving instructor; you should enter this profession, unless you have other plans to earn a living.'

Her encouragement and praise got me thinking and I enquired at various schools about what it would take to become a driving instructor. They too gave me more encouragement, especially because I could teach in English and German; that seemed to be a great advantage. There were no rules for becoming an instructor; you just had to have your car converted so it had dual controls for your own safety. There were no tests to be written. If you could explain to a total stranger how to operate an automobile you could call yourself a driving instructor!

I took a chance and signed up with one of the schools I had contacted and became one of their instructors. They provided me with the clientele and I did my very best to be a good teacher.

After six months I had the confidence to open a driving school of my own. My students were happy with my instructions; they in turn became drivers who had the confidence to be on the road and master the traffic that seemed to increase from week to week.

Together with several other schools we formed the Driving School Association of Southern California and I became a charter member. Today I am the only charter member left; everyone else has to be visited at the graveside. Our association initiated rules and regulations to operate a driving school in California and the Department of Motor Vehicles supervises our industry.

As luck would have it, many of my clientele came from the movie industry and I instructed famous stars or members of their family and household. The film industry does not consist only of stars, but there were producers, directors, writers, composers, etc. Teddy Donaldson was my very first celebrity I had the privilege to instruct, and Ving Rhames was the last one before my retirement. In between I taught Michael Caine, Judy Light, Sheena Easton, Juliette Mills and Jim Sheridan, just to name a few.

One of the brightest stars to outshine everybody was a young lady by the name of Sue Grosz, whose name I changed to Sue Herrmann. Yes, I am referring to my wife. I met Sue at a private party and she told me about her adventures in China, where she and her parents had survived the Holocaust, and from where she had come to America recently.

Her boss had urged her to learn to drive and I assured her that I would be delighted to teach her the art of driving an automobile and enrolled her in my school and scheduled her first lesson. Sue was not only a bright student, but she was a very attractive young lady, good looking, well-versed and fun to be together with. We became very good friends and I dated her and we did what young people do, we went out dancing, to the movies, to private parties, etc.

One Friday evening, Erev Sabbath, we went to the Fairfax Temple to attend Friday night services. We sat down in one of the seats and in front of us was a prayer book to follow the services. As we opened the book at the start of the services, an old used *mezuzah* fell out from between the pages, the kind you normally attach to the doorpost of your home. G'd had given us a hint that we should form a homestead and thus our engagement time began!

Later on when we got married, I promised Sue I would refund the tuition fee she had paid me for the driving lessons with one proviso; I would pay her back one dollar yearly. I figured it would take twenty years of refunds and I would have proof that our marriage would last. Sue passed away on 21 May 2001 – we were married for nearly fifty-two years!

Letters

A few years after the war ended, I received a large package of letters from Willi and Claire Herrmann, who were living in Cali, Colombia, South America as well as from my Aunt and Uncle Marthl and Willi Griessmeier. These were all the letters they had received from my parents between early June 1939 until they left Nordhausen in September 1942 and when they were deported from Theresienstadt on 4 November 1943.

As grateful as I was that these two families had collected these letters for me, it was terribly painful to read them, even though they were written years ago. Since many of these letters were subject to censorship, my parents had to be extremely careful in what they were reporting, especially in the letters sent to Colombia. From the beginning of the war all correspondence had to be submitted in open envelopes.

To understand what they were trying to say, one had to read between the lines. For example, they were not officially allowed to report that they could no longer own radios or telephones, or that they were not permitted to read newspapers. They were condemned to live on the lowest food ration cards and were exposed to all kinds of abuse. If they reported any problems, they would have been sent to the nearest concentration camp.

For my parents, the psychological stress must have been tremendous – saying goodbye to so many of their friends and relatives – yet they were caught like rats in a cage, with no immediate help in sight.

There were no more doctors in town and friends had to help each other as best as they could. My mother had a nerve inflammation in her left leg and it took weeks to heal. Friends came to help and tried to treat her as best as they knew how with medical knowledge they had from earlier days.

I will not bore you with family correspondence but will reproduce excerpts from their letter describing their silver wedding anniversary and their last four postcards addressed to the Griessmeiers in Munich.

My dear Griessmeiers,

We were happy to receive your dear letter and thank you for the good wishes on the occasion of our silver wedding anniversary. We were honoured from all sides. Our room was a real flower garden. It pays to have such a festivity and forget the daily routine. We received lots of mail but the letters of our dear ones abroad were missing, especially from our son, Kurt. Through a Red Cross letter we heard that Kurt works in a glove factory and that all our dear ones are OK.

Harri

My dears,

Now the silver wedding anniversary is behind us. It was such a harmonious and beautiful day. We will never forget it in our whole lives. We received so much love from everyone and it really touched us. Your words and wishes did us good and to top it off, the fact that everything was wrapped in butter was simply fantastic! A thousand thanks for everything!

Early at 7:30 am our remaining relatives and friends surprised us, and they all came with some gifts. They brought their own food and we all enjoyed a nice brew of coffee together. Everybody sacrificed his or her last coffee beans for this occasion.

It was the most comfortable and nicest hour of the day. One's life has become so modest and one has to thank G'd for every quiet hour one can live under one's own roof.

Our good friend Ida Seelig, who lives in the old age home at Frankfurt/Main sent us a wonderful poem for our anniversary. The next day we received a postcard from her, in which she says farewell to us. She had been told that she had to undertake her 'great trip into the unknown'. It is too gruesome! It continues daily! It is too gruesome!

Harri's sister Grete Frank, nee Herrmann, now living in Amsterdam,

Holland also writes in great despair and unhappiness. I am afraid she too will have to leave there.
Rosa

I too want to send you, my dear ones, my heartiest greetings and many thanks for all your love. We did indeed have some wonderful hours, which we will never forget. If only dear G'd could hold his protective hand over us!
Once more my fervent greetings,
Your old faithful
Lea Moses

The following card was written one day before departure from Nord-hausen to 'destination unknown':

18th September 1942

My dear ones,
Many thanks for your last loving letter. Let me assure you, we will never forget you. We are feeling very downhearted, but we will try to keep strong. Saturday morning we will be leaving. Give a thousand regards to all our dear ones abroad, whenever you will write to them.
For you I wish that your boy would survive the war in good health.
Let me take you in my arms once more and kiss you with all my heart, with much love,
Yours,
Rosa

Farewell my dear ones! May G'd protect us and give us strength.
With deep felt love,
Yours,
Oma

My dear ones,
We were very happy with your recent lines and want to send you once more our heartiest farewell.
Please, give all our dear ones, especially our dear son, notice of our departure, so he will know what became of us.
For your boy we wish you the best of the best. Remain in good health, with hearty regards and kisses,
Your ever-loving
Harri

Lea Moses was called 'Oma' by her grandchildren and adopted the name as her regular signature. The previous lines were the last written by Lea Moses before her death on 15 May 1943 in the ghetto Theresienstadt.

Theresienstadt, 26th June 1943

My dears!
We are in good health and hope the same of you. Letters and little packages are permissible and are delivered promptly.
Mother Lea unfortunately died on May 15th, 1943.
How is your son Kurt? We hope to hear from you real soon.
We embrace you and kiss you, with much love,
Yours,
Rosa and Harri

27th October 1943

My dear ones,
We are extremely happy with your packages and thank you ever so much. The grits and the marmalade tasted especially good.
My dear Harri, unfortunately, had to undergo a very serious operation. I was in great worry, but thank G'd, he is on the way to recovery.
In the hope to hear from you regularly, I'll take you in my arms heartily,
Your ever so grateful,
Rosa

(Harri Herrmann had to undergo a gallbladder operation under the most primitive conditions in the so-called hospital of the ghetto Theresienstadt, where everything was missing as far as supplies were concerned, but where they had some of the most famous surgeons in the world!)

Theresienstadt, 4th November 1943

My dears,
I am in receipt of your package from 25th of October 1943.
Letter will follow.
Rosa Herrmann

There was a note from Martha Griessmeier that this was the last reply
for a package; after that there were no more replies.

CONCLUSION

EDITH STILL LIVES in Kirkcaldy in the county of Fife in Scotland. Kurt lives in Los Angeles, California and I live in Johannesburg, South Africa.

Through writing this book, we hope that these stories from the Holocaust will help us never to forget what the Jewish people suffered in this terrible time. For Kurt's son, Robert and daughter-in-law, Barbara, and his grandsons Joshua and Jonathan, it is the story of their family history. For our children, David and Adrienne, son-in-law, Ian, and our grandchildren, Aharon, Zahava, Liora and Ayala Bogatie, this book, which has been written with so much love, will hopefully be handed down to their families with pride in years to come.